Dancing with Empty Prams

Title: Dancing with Empty Prams / Susan Austin
ISBN 9780645089387
Cover design: Jen Lorrimar-Shanks

Publisher: Walleah Press
23 Hobart Road
South Launceston
Tasmania, Australia 7249
www.walleahpress.com.au
ralph.wessman@walleahpress.com.au

Dancing with Empty Prams

Susan Austin

CONTENTS

1.

2.

3.

1.

The resting kettle

We try not to bring work home
but tonight,
after a quick tofu and veggie stir-fry,
Patrick heads to the study to write his keynote
for the International Conference of Aquatic Sciences.

I open my laptop on the kitchen table,
go over the monthly profit and loss figures,
update the shop's inventory.
We both love our jobs but ...

he is rational,
    social,
        gregarious,
            sleeps hot,
                loves aircon,
                    eats meat,
                        can totally relax in a messy house.
Me?
I'm emotional,
    introverted,
        serious,
            sleep cold,
                hate aircon,
                    am strictly vegan,
                        need order (and maybe a bit more order).

In a billion other ways we're opposites.
He thinks bread should be stored in a paper bag or it will go soggy,
I think it should be stored in a plastic bag or it will go stale.

The one thing we profoundly agree on is   sustainable living.
It propels Patrick's research.
It drives me to supply this town with eco-friendly provisions.

My shop is 'Ripe Earth Foods'.
It's been my passion, really my life, for 5 years.
And it's thriving.
Just saying that makes me shiver with pride (& yes, he left the aircon on).

Sometimes the amount of work needed to keep the show running
threatens to suffocate me like a wool blanket on a humid night –

there's the hiring, training and supervising of staff,
building relationships with suppliers (more than fifty now),
maintaining a vibrant shop profile on Facebook and Twitter,
periodically re-arranging and re-decorating the shop,
operating the Saturday market stall,
keeping on top of the books,
the payroll …
and all the extra jobs I never knew existed …

until I decided
that opening an organic, low-waste shop in the heart of the Bay
was what I needed to do to help save the planet.

Want to break for a cuppa? I ask,
leaning wearily against his study door.
Patrick follows me out, perches on a kitchen stool
while I steep two cups of vanilla rooibos tea.

We sit and sip,
gaze at the steam floating up from the resting kettle,
ask shallow questions about work,
half listen to each other,
when really our thoughts are still in our laptops.

Ready

Lately, the question of kids keeps insisting.
Would kids like these? I ponder
as I check the quality of the sultanas
and the size of the sulphur-free dried apricots.
I notice every baby and toddler who enters the store –
strapped to chests, pushed in prams,
staggering on cupid legs, hands held.

Having a baby would give Patrick and me a common project –
instead of always hot-stepping in separate directions
     a baby
would force us to dance together.

I crave cuddles, joy,
that mother-child bond I had with my mum
as she read Golden Books aloud to me on her knee
(oh, to enjoy The Poky Little Puppy again!)

There must be more to life than selling pesticide-free produce.

I've never felt more ready
to slow things down,
hand over the reins,
sit on the plush tangerine mat in our airy lounge-room
and squeeze a squeaky giraffe
beside a baby
of my own.

Mother's work

He's given his keynote address,
the shop's in a steady rhythm, stocktake done,
so I begin my quest.

First step: convince Patrick
that having children would be a good thing to do,
while harbouring doubts about my narrow pelvis, stretch marks
and the desirability of having my breasts sucked dry for years.

He likes his routine, his current life, I know,
but he relents
to keep me happy.
I sense, deep down, he really wants to be a dad,
and he'll be a great one, I'm certain.

Time is not on my side.
I need to get to work researching
the science and the art of procreation.

Soon   I'm monitoring mucus,
measuring basal temperature,
interrupting work at two pm to dip strips into urine,
testing for LH (Luteinizing Hormone) surges,
plotting goddess and master:
ovulation.

Night after night in the fertile window
I pull out risqué underwear,
forgo movie dates with friends,
the latest David Attenborough docos and early nights
for the task of enticing my sperm-laden partner to party
regardless of something as fickle as   desire.

I raise my legs for twenty minutes after sex
then navigate the perilous Two Week Wait,
trying not to analyse every bodily symptom.

I roll baby names around in my mind when driving,
buy both tampons and pregnancy tests as D-day approaches
only to pick myself up after each bloody disappointment

to try it all again (with some well-researched variations)
ten days later.

I put other plans on hold,
not knowing if my efforts will ever be known as
        mother's work
or, in sad retrospect, be seen as a delusion
that I could ever grow and push a new person
into this bright, precarious world.

If a pregnant belly does not eventuate,
if the spare room remains achingly unnecessary,
then this mother's love will be formless, invisible,
        wasted.

An ulterior motive is not an aphrodisiac

We discover
it's so much easier to have sex

when you don't have to.

Each time

Trying for months but each time
the subtle signs of PMT
leave an unwanted crimson messenger in their wake.

So I can't be blamed for giving in
to the cab-sav on the bench near the toaster
as Friday washes me against the rocks
of the Two Week Wait.

The grapes help me escape
the ninety-per-cent-certain disappointment,
yet I can't quite float
on a mellow vintage raft
without the needling doubt
that inside

      there's a grand race occurring,
      an egg-and-sperm hide-and-seek,
      a genetic tango

which I am poisoning
with fermented impatience.

Weight of expectation

Ovulation is not patient
nor its agenda malleable.
In the bathroom at the shop this morning
the testing strip is positive –
my LH has surged.
Tonight I can't concentrate
on Agatha Christie,
impatient for the sound of Patrick coming.

He's been at the Sunshine Coast campus all week,
lecturing on seaweed,
sustainable algae cultivation and nutraceuticals.
Other times he goes to Bribie Island,
bunkers down near the one-thousand-litre tanks he's filled
with his beloved *Asparagopsis taxiformis*.

Methane is twenty-eight times more climate-wrecking
than carbon dioxide.
Patrick's big discovery is
that a compound, bromoform,
(see I do listen more than superficially, sometimes)
in his darling red seaweed
knocks out the stomach bugs
that cause each cow to belch out
over seventy kilograms of the deadly stuff a year.

I went with him once to Moffat Beach.
Him, sexy in his short-sleeve wetsuit,
teaching me which treasure to scoop up —
dusky pink globular ribbons
whose essence gives the sea its smell.
His mission is
to find a way to grow it large-scale
so everyone can eat low-carbon steak.

He gently places male and female plants together in tanks,
experimenting with the best conditions to grow it fast,
feeling the weight of industry expectation.
For his beloved algae
he adjusts temperature, light,
nutrients, carbon dioxide concentrations.

Come home, Patrick,
     gently place us together
     weigh my hungry expectations.
Adjust me.

Flatness

I can see my friend Sylvia is uncomfortable
explaining to me why I haven't seen her much lately,
telling me about her morning sickness,
how she's been tired and nauseous in the evenings,
usually in bed by eight-thirty —
... but anyway, what have you been up to? she quickly asks,
      too aware
            of her belly's warm bump
                  facing my enduring flatness.

Name games

Every ad break during *Dancing with The Stars*
I twirl around baby names —
a game I've always liked to play
in quiet moments since I was a kid.

Don't torture yourself, Patrick says, after joining in for a bit,
dishing Danny or Billy
but saying *Zach's okay*,
before finding the game too raw, too sad.

I'm hyperactive for some reason,
makes a change from irritated, tired.

This week, leading up to my period,
                    tough.

So many indications —
insatiable hunger,
nausea,
no routine pimples,
emotions helter-skelter.
Could Pre-Menstrual Tension really make me feel this weird?

Whenever I'm not suitably distracted,
the same narrative,
the same self-diagnostics,
take hold in my head.
What does this sign mean? And this one?
A heart-flutter thought — am I finally, actually pregnant?

Five long days or more
before I can expect relief
from my oscillating conclusions,
my useless self-lecturing against wishful thinking,
stubborn fantasy.

When it arrives,
I feel betrayed,
angry,
stupid …
deceived once again
by my untrustworthy intuition,
my ever-more distant body.

Bloody period

Pudgy legs

Have you ever noticed
how many cute babies there are
in airports?

As we wait at our gate,
I watch the ones around me.

A toddler in the row facing me
wears a mock miniskirt
attached to a blue stripy top.
The outfit hovers above pudgy legs.
She stands, wobbling, on the seat,
grips the backrest,
gurgles back at the adoring adults.

On the plane
I chew envy-salted peanuts.
I even long to be
the parent
        wrestling
                the screaming baby
                        up the back.

Blossoming

I find some solace
seeing new life sprout on our baby fruit trees.

My nickname as a kid was Fruit-bat.

Six years in and we finally get round to planting
a little orchard in our weed-dominated backyard.

As the days warm and lengthen,
the Imperial and Emperor mandarin trees flush with glossy leaves.

The grafted (and expensive) Bowen mango seedling
is the first to produce perfect green gifts —
                    each one plump and curvy as a foetus.

The lychee trees' flimsy branches
display two clusters of seven blossoms each.

The Lady Finger banana flaunts five leaves, big as baby-blankets,
but is beaten in height by its Cavendish brother.

The twig of a mulberry, after a month of sulking,
finally musters up three shiny lime-green shoots.

The Super-Dwarf Sunset nectarine proudly shows off
its single tiny nectarine-to-be.

I reach out to it, smiling,
but my gentle touch knocks it to the ground.

Hope

Every afternoon before dinner
I stand, hose in hand, showering water droplets
onto our young providers-to-be,
allowing my breath to slow as I watch
the water cascade over leaves, branches,
meld into the thirsty soil.

In gloomy moments
when emptiness torments,
I cast my mind
over our growing garden
and the baskets of fruit
I hope to harvest
each summer
should things continue as they are.

Boutique weeds

I wake at 5am. Can't get back to sleep.
My breasts are definitely aching, different.

In the space between not knowing,
mind jumps in,
steps me through what I want to happen.
It's hard to rein in excitement when it's been unleashed.

Who will I tell and when?
I imagine the incredible relief and joy
of seeing the blue line appear
and of being able to tell Patrick, for once, the news he wants to hear.
The next day – phone calls to my sister and parents,
at six weeks – my good friends and the rest of the family,
at three months, after the all-clear – everyone can know.

It means I'll be finishing work about May.
I'll have to work out what salary to offer Evie
to entice her
to step into my shoes
and I'll be able to buy bags of books about
pregnancy, baby sleep routines, child-rearing.
I'll lash out on some angel-soft hand-knitted baby clothes
like those I stroked wistfully in a boutique in Mapleton that day
but had to leave behind.

Each day after my period due-date
passes slowly.
The pregnancy test gives a clear negative reading
but there is still no period.
Hope grows like weeds pushing through the cracks,

until my period turns up,
lazy,
a week late,
felling the weeds like a machete.

Been watching too many documentaries?

Maybe my eggs have heard the scientist's predictions
of arctic ice melt, climate disaster —
taken the compassionate option
and bailed out.

Stimulating jobs

I'm keeping the folate manufacturers in work
and the makers of preconception multivitamins.
I'm doing all the right things

                              aren't I?

Bleeding

Despite what you might think,
the day the blood starts flowing
is not the worst day of the cycle.

It is bitter, yes,
but also a momentary resolution,
an answer to the unbearable uncertainty,
the what's-going-on-with-my-body preoccupation.

No matter where I am, what I'm doing,
my body is there too, teasing me
with food cravings, mood swings,
abdominal pains and strange sensations ...
yes, the usual monthly signs,
but impossible not to get my hopes up each time
despite the foolishness of it ...

so when the blood starts flowing,
there is relief,
sadness
and sometimes despair

but at least there is an understanding again
between me and my body

and for a while there is nothing to do
but bleed.

Action stations

I read all I can about techniques to boost fertility.
I need something more than supplements.
Acupuncture gets mentioned a lot on forums.
Doctor Google says it improves blood flow
to the ovaries
and the endometrium
which can increase the thickness of the uterus lining.

In another breath Doctor Google also says
there is no real evidence
of it improving chances of conception
or curing infertility.

The one conclusive statement seems to be
that it reduces stress.
I have no idea how lying down
on a hard bed
enduring needles stuck into you all over
reduces stress

but it can't hurt to try,   can it?

If trying to conceive naturally,
Doctor Google recommends weekly treatment
for around twelve weeks.

The acupuncturist has a waitlist.
I add my name —
wait.

Focusing

I've dropped down to four days a week at work,
promoting Evie to fill my role on the other two.
I outsource payroll and accounts.

Hope that any built-up cortisol in my body
dissipates
as I start to breathe easier,
rest,
stretch,
write in my journal.

Two more boxes of ovulation predictor kits arrived today —
we're all stocked up.

Got a new game plan
for marshalling those reluctant sperm.

Cracking open

Fuck having kids,
Patrick yells, storming off.

Okay, so I'd given him
a bit of a death stare
when he told me he'd be away for work next week
on Tuesday and Wednesday —
Day Sixteen and Day Seventeen —
even though we'd agreed on a plan:
to have sex the morning after
a positive ovulation test
(usually happens around then).

I've got no choice! he defends himself,
lectures are locked in!
That's unfortunate, I say
        and that gets him going.
We can't have kids anyway!
Anger, the child of powerlessness.
            What's the point in trying?

I try to distract myself
with Facebook on my phone,
but can't deal with all the
friends' baby photos
and the 'listen-to-what-cute-thing-my-boy-said-today' posts.

The reality gap hurts.

I crack open a beer,
sip the bitter ale.

And so another egg falls...

through the arguments,
twelve months of trying,
laboured lovemaking,
me tracking   temperatures
                         LH surges
                            mucus,
searching for
          the right time,

Patrick fully wanting, then half-wanting.

With that level of ambivalence 'motivating' his sperm
what chance do they have
of forging fearlessly
through cervix, uterus, the endless fallopian tubes
to reach their briefly loitering target?

The signs are right, the planets align –
another egg falls,
only this time,
this month,
as my fingers stroke supple skin
he airs his views:
          I don't really want children
          I only said yes
          because you wanted me to.

The trying stops.

Fingers retract as though bitten.

He fears change.
I've always known he is risk averse
(another of our many differences).

I sense a selfishness,
a narrow view
            of what makes life worthwhile.

I am lost
like the sperm, the egg,
planets off kilter.
What was already outside of my control
spins further away.

Will there be any more
fourteendaysafterovulationwaits?

Will there be any more
watchingforsymptomsthatcouldbePMTcouldbemore?
Will there be any more weighing up of baby names?

Will there be a future for us together?

Backs turn.　　I think all this
in furious silence.

Curl into myself.
Call for sleep to soothe me.

Say goodbye to the egg
falling quietly into the night.

Low levels

No period.
Still no period.
No blue line.
Still no blue line.

Sitting beside the GP's desk, I sob.
Seven days late and a big fight with Patrick over having a baby
            and I just need to know.

Waiting for the blood test results,
I am not coping.
Call him home from work,
insist on talking,
finding our way out of wreckage.
Do we stay together if we want such different things?

In the midst of this fiery, tear-filled discussion
the GP calls: *It's positive   but the levels are low.*

What does that mean? Am I pregnant or not?

Yes, but it may not last   caution clipping every syllable.

Crying uncontrollably,
I tell her I have never been so stressed in my life,
Is that what is putting this baby at risk?

No, it has no impact, just wait and see, we'll retest in a few days.

Our relationship issues evaporate
because there are tears of relief in Patrick's eyes.
He is so happy I am pregnant
and we both learn
      he does want children.

Yet it is perilous ...

and within hours it is over.

Bleeding.
Clotted, heavy
bleeding.

A chemical pregnancy,
an early miscarriage.

Shock and sorrow rock me
but there is a silver lining —

our relationship crisis has been solved
by this scarlet agglomeration of cells

gurgling and swirling down the toilet's throat.

Pinned

Today I begin acupuncture.

So it's come to this, I think,

stretched out on a thin bench
beneath fluoro lights,
pins sticking out of my tender
        feet, wrists, stomach, scalp,

each taking their turn to sting.

Left alone for fifteen minutes,
I listen to the heater's hum,
hope this mysterious practice —
turning the body into a pin-cushion —
soothes my internal, subconscious hesitations.

Delicate process

The start of another Two Week Wait.
Already I am scrutinising my actions,
wishing I hadn't sat out with the mosquitos for an hour last night,
slapping my arms as I watched Patrick play semi-finals basketball.
They say the fertilised egg needs tranquillity.

Yesterday I felt suffocated
by all the things that need doing at the shop.
I could feel my heart pounding
and much as I tried to regulate my breathing,
I know stress hormones
were running rampant within.

In bed last night I had nightmares, as I often do,
people attacking with knives, me stabbing back in self-defence.
Maybe I slept too hot, had too many layers on.

Maybe the slapping, the stress, the nightmares or the heat
have scared away the sperm,
unsettled the egg,
or otherwise disrupted
the delicate process
that might   just might
be going on inside.

God's plan

In 'Caleb's Crossing', I am strangely heartened to read
that the fictional female character, in the late 1600's,
had fertility problems too.

*We had, after more than two years, begun to resign ourselves
to the possibility that God would not bless us with issue,* she said.

How much simpler back then, to accept things as God's plan.

Now you can choose
between acceptance and the 'divine' promise of IVF

that is, if you've moved on from denial.

Bloody period

Barren

Playing the board-game, Articulate.
Amy holds the playing card over her pregnant belly,
gives clues excitedly as the sand funnels through the egg-timer.

A woman who can't have children!
Like a desert where nothing grows!

Barren!　　　Grace chimes in, her two-year-old curled in her lap.

Yes, that's it!　Smiles, quickly moves on to the next clue.

I sit there, a sudden ache in my abdomen.

That's me you are talking about —
　　　　a desert where nothing grows?

Complimentary

Another business trip
where I'm able to drink
the complimentary wine
on the flight home.

The smooth merlot
softens and warms my throat
with its consolation.

Happy accidents

My weekday cashier, Misty, brings in
celebratory choc-beetroot cupcakes.
Jade, Evie, I have some news!   She grins madly.

I want to say —
I'm happy you got pregnant
by accident
a month before you'd planned to start trying,
I really am.
But let me take you on a journey.
I'd just like to give you a glimpse
of this see-saw I've been on,
this pretence of a normal life,
this invisible, private, cyclic endeavour
that each month
for the past twenty-four months
has led to blood, disappointment, more blood,
                 despair.

All played out
against the backdrop
of daily temperature testing from day ten
(each morning, inserting the thermometer is the first act)
then after the first morning wee,
I hold on for at least four hours,
test my urine about the same time each day,

no matter which one of you employees are waiting
to talk to me about leave requests or sweet potato prices,
no matter how stuffy and unpleasant the bathroom is.

Just imagine the sexy, spontaneous,
lusciousness of sex
being pinned to a calendar
dictating when
and in what positions,
no matter how big a day we've had,
no matter what visitors are staying in the room next door,
no matter if one of us isn't in the mood,
no matter if one of us is sick,
time after time after time again,
until sex is a chore,
until Patrick feels like nothing more than an inadequate sperm dispenser,
until business trips and holidays and conferences
clash with the fertile window
causing tears and arguments and another month lost,
until I feel like I am always dripping semen,
until I begin to curse my body for not co-operating,
curse him for not letting us start trying years earlier
(he had to finish that brilliant PhD first, of course).

Some months, during the Two Week Wait, symptoms appear
leading me, against my better judgement, to believe.

Between customers and online orders my mind slides softly
towards visions of borrowing baby gear,
choosing prams,
thoughts of Patrick's joy when I break the news,
plotting the months til I can walk out of here
and take as much guilt-free time off as I like.
Those months are the worst, when it's hardest to bounce back,
when we blame ourselves for letting hope slip too far inside the door.

Each time I gently, or irritably, break the news about my bleeding,
I fret about my vaginal mucus,
the backward tilt of my uterus,
my stress levels,
our future.

Instead I coo   *Congratulations, Misty! How wonderful!!*

ask all the right questions,
take a cupcake,
try to wash it down my closed-tight throat
with a cup of scalding chai.

Whale watching

I.
Evie and Misty are managing the market pack-up.

I've shouted us a special treat —
Patrick and I will play tourists,
go whale watching,
something we haven't done since
just after moving to the Bay.

He's often in the ocean for work,
seen whales plenty of times before,
but might enjoy sharing his knowledge,
talking about something tangible,
something other than uselessly trying to make a baby.
I look forward to learning and watching
and not being responsible for anything.

After an hour of cruising,
soaking up the breeze, the salt-spray
and the sparkling light,
we come across two mothers and their calves.
The boat drifts   we all hold our breaths and stare,
                    mesmerized,
as they twist and dive,   playing.

Acrobats of the ocean —
one pair slap the water with their pectoral fins,
the mother performs a mighty peduncle throw and slap.

One calf is especially energetic —
breaching powerfully   again and again
as its mother's tail creates an exquisite upward arc
                    before slowly rolling under the surface.

Their eerie songs cast a spell on us
through the boat's underwater hydrophones.
The alchemy of their mother-baby communication
leaves me reeling.

II.
After they judge we are satisfied with the spectacle
the tour leaders cruise us away,
head to a different area,
serve us banana muffins and cups of over-stewed tea,
point out plumes of spray   in the distance.

We slow to a stop
when the captain spots
a pair of green sea turtles.
He explains the courtship dance the male is performing
as he tries to woo the female.
They swim,   spin   and glide,
          large dome shells pirouetting.

The male starts to mount the female
but as his head clears the surface
he looks across and sees us
and in an instant
they both dive straight down
deep
leaving only a ripple.

We head back to the marina as the sun starts to go down,
glossing K'gari with a tangelo glow.
It feels so romantic.
I sidle closer to Patrick,
will him
to put his arm around me

but he doesn't.

Lost years

The end of a long year draws near.
We don't know what we're doing wrong
          if anything.

We don't know what to try next.

Everyone tells us to relax.

After two years, we begin to work out how.

We pick up some shreds of hope
and continue on
          as lightly as we can.

Still on the runway

We are stuck in a plane,
waiting for the lightning warnings to finish,
for the hailstones on the tarmac to melt.
Rocked by gusts of wind,
we watch the rain dance across the thick window panes.

We wait for the other planes ahead of us in the queue.

Then the warning sirens begin again.
We wait for the next storm to pass.

It's late afternoon, Christmas day.
Some call friends and family –
Go to dinner without us, they urge.
Some snooze, Christmas ham and puddings heavy in their bellies.
I smile at the toddler-girl who waddles up and down the aisle,
making friends.
I text Grace *Merry Christmas.*
She had her second child three days ago.

I've shed my tears this month.

Last night, unable to sleep,
unsettled, I thought back to two years earlier
when I was in the same house,
unwrapping presents with nieces and nephews

around the same tree,
and the hope I had then that next Christmas
we would have a child of our own.

They let us off the plane to get some food,
to wait inside the airport lounge,
where I attempt another conversation.
As usual, I fail to engage Patrick
in a discussion of *what next*.

He avoids the question —
his unhappy refrain
                    I'm tired of it all.

We resolve to talk about it later, not here,
where he glances around uncomfortably
at any mention of taboo words.

In between watching lightning lacerate the sky behind the glass
and trying to ignore a woman making loud calls on her mobile
beside me,
I notice my stomach drop
at the thought of what he might say —
or not say —
when we do begin to talk.

Sunset from the window seat

The sun sets through my window,
slowly imbuing the cloud-layered sky
with stunning pink and gold.

We might not have a baby, I think,
but we've got each other

and in this moment,
that's enough.

Symbols

At work, Friday morning, on hold to an organic dairy supplier,
the recorded message cheerily asks:
> *Did you know the Easter bunny represents fertility?*

I'd just finished eating my Easter bunny the night before
and was getting my period today
as I sat at the end of the phone line
thinking, *it doesn't bloody represent fertility to me.*

All those little eggs I'd eaten over Easter
didn't mean much either
except
> *unfertilised*
>> or
> *failure to implant.*

Orange juice advice

In Sydney a month later for the National Organics Conference,
my elderly hosts
ask if I'm planning to have children —

Yes, I think so.

The husband kindly warns me
Don't leave it too late,
giving me multiple reasons why.

Oh stop it, his wife says,
she has to live her life first.

Yes but just don't leave it too late, he persists, meaning well

and I want to tell them
how hard and how long we've been trying,
how much we want children
and how my period is two days late
but I remain discreet — I have already shared my woes
with too many friends —
and I can sense my period is on its way.
The next morning it arrives
before I sit down with them for breakfast
and sip the glass of orange juice he's squeezed for me.

Over our Weetbix conversation, they go on
believing
that I'm preoccupied with
     living my life first.

Two years, seven months

I remember when six months of trying seemed like a long time.

Splashing out

My french-fry-feeding fingers
leave oily prints on my wine glass.
I savour the aroma
of a finely-balanced Tasmanian sauvignon blanc.

It's not good for the budget, this pregnancy game —
every bottle bought could be my last
so each month, at the bottle-shop,
I splash out on quality.

I secretly enjoy the fact
that I can take an expensive bottle
to dinner with pregnant friends
knowing that it is all mine,
a crisp, clean, citrus-tinged
consolation.

Breaking news

Once again I get my period while I'm away,
this time meeting with suppliers in Brisbane.

Do I break the news to Patrick by text message?
Or make it the first bit of news to report
when he collects me from the airport?

Or wait until we are home in bed
and I can hug him
and tell him with the warmth of my body
that I love him
no matter what?

By-product

I serve a customer at the cash register
who has a baby fixed to her chest
with a large tie-dyed wrap-around scarf.

The baby, with a shock of black hair,
stares wondrously at me with huge eyes
as I pack her mother's bulk-buy containers
into her hessian bag   with some force.
After I hand over the receipt I catch myself
glowering in her happy-mother face.

She leaves the shop and I slump
onto the desk in the back office
and confess to Evie –

> *I'm worried I've become*
> *bitter*
> *and twisted.*

She trills   *Yes, probably.*
> *You know, bitterness is the by-product*
> *of a failure to process raw emotions.*

I want to scream at her triteness
and cry
but I go back out

unpack a box of bananas.

Pinned again

The pin sticking into my scalp is really hurting
        or maybe it's just me?

Lying on the acupuncturist's bench,
in a room by myself,
under persistent fluoro lights,
unable to move,
when even curling my toes causes sharp stabs,
I start to cry.
A tsunami of tears
runs down my face,
into my ears,
unstoppable.
I would wipe them away
but both my hands are pinned.

I cry about my bitterness,
about the loss I feel when
I see a pram in the street,
about the effort it takes to visit friends
who have kids and more on the way,
about the present I didn't buy for Sylvia's baby,
about the irony of taking part in marches
that demanded the right
for women to control their own bodies,
their own fertility,
about the double contraception we used for years.

The doctor comes back in after fifteen minutes
and still I can't stop.
He is kind, gentle.
We talk about bitterness
and he tells me it may be a stage,
like anger can be a stage of grief
and I know that makes sense
but I can't stop crying.

Afterwards I sit in the little waiting room
trying to compose myself.
I pay, bite my lip when my eyes start to water,
keep small talk to a minimum,
rush to my car.

At home lying on the couch,
the phone rings.
I answer with a soft   *Hello.*

It's Parks and Wildlife.
He asks if my mother's there.
I must sound like a child.

I pause, not sure what to say,
then respond, simply *No.*

I'll call back later then, he says
and I hang up, bewildered by sorrow —

        there is no child, nor mother, in this house.

Dancing with the Stars

After a crap day at work,
when the cash register died,
the milk delivery didn't come until late afternoon
and I endured a headache all day
while trying to placate annoyed customers,
I veg on the couch with the remote.
At least *Dancing with the Stars* is on,
my guilty, reality-TV addiction.

My favourite dances are the cha-cha-cha, the salsa and the tango.
Patrick usually watches something else on the iPad, headphones on.
I tried to convince him a few times, in our earlier years,
to go to ballroom dancing classes with me.
He joked about having two left feet
and firmly refused.
So I satisfy myself
with this weekly fix,
        watching others dancing.

Floundering

If I compare myself
to all my friends who fell pregnant easily
and those who have lapped me
while I'm still floundering behind the starting line,
I wallow in envy and self-pity.

If I compare myself to the few women I know
who want children but don't even have partners,
or my brassica supplier who has young children
but just lost her husband to brain cancer,
I stumble into guilt — feel I don't have the right
to complain.

I learn
comparisons are not useful,

pain cannot be argued away.

Meeting with my marketing consultant

Ooo Jade, I didn't know you were pregnant! she gushes,
touching my arm, excited.

I know instantly what's happening.
This new dress I bought
to cheer myself up
gathers under the bust.
I put on a few kilos in case my thinness
was sending the wrong physiological message.
Combined with my tall-girl slouch,
my belly must be a little pronounced ...

No, I said, *I'm not, it must be the dress ...*

       unless you're psychic, I think, as it's the day my period is due.

Maybe you know something I don't ...

She's embarrassed   *... silly thing to do ...* apologising profusely.

It's fine, I say, trying to grin reassuringly
through my gritted teeth.

Is this as close as I will get?
A pregnancy-dress pretender?

I banish it to the back of my wardrobe,
never to be worn again.

She was not psychic.

The dance

Bitter Disappointment hands me over to Hope
who steps me through some spirited salsa.

Anxiety takes over, stumbling with two left feet.
He leads me through some ungraceful pirouettes
before passing me back to Bitter Disappointment.

In his sharp black coat and tailored trousers,
Bitter Disappointment waltzes me,
cupping his right hand
against my shoulder blade — a solid, guiding force.

I take a short break on the bench,
watching all the other dancers
before stepping up, finding Hope's arms again,
jiving comfortably across the floor.
Anxiety cuts in, unsettling me
with his lack of rhythm
then before long
Bitter Disappointment taps him on the shoulder,
sends him to the sidelines.

I am becoming skilled at this cycle,
getting to know each partner,
especially this dark-suited one
who dances close and grips tight.

He has much to teach me.

Self-education

Three books on IVF in three weeks.

Had to renew a few over the phone with the library.
Who in this town is taking note of my new interest
and all those titles waiting for me,   with my name sticking out,
on the Holds shelf?

Two more books on IVF in a further two weeks.

Had my fill of contradictory advice and tips on managing the turmoil.
Wish I could be reading books about pregnancy or escapist chick-lit.

Information gathering

I'm devouring an ocean of articles and books.
     He's the research scientist ...
          won't even read one measly pamphlet.
     What's that about?

No wine tonight

Am all prepared.
Don't want to read any more info on IVF.

Want to get on with this.
Too much talk not enough action.

Waiting for the specialist appointment,
one last shot at getting pregnant naturally.

Another good effort,
perfect timing
but once again we may as well
have drunk ourselves silly.

2.

Turning to Doctor Google

Fuck.
Fuck! Fuck! Fuck!
I swear and sob
and sob and sob.

The sperm results —
envelope ripped open in front of me on the dining-room table,
white and black A4 report laid flat.

Our GPs got the ball rolling,
the tests done
a week before we see the fertility specialist.

Twenty tabs active in the web browser on my laptop —
the last hour spent with Doctor Google
answered my questions — we're fucked.
Why why why did I request a copy?

Ididn'twantthisItcan'tbehappeningItcan'tbetrue.
He's so fit, so healthy, so MASCULINE.

What am I going to do? Does this mean IVF for sure? Do I stay with
him if it means we can't have kids? Do we need a sperm donor? A
SPERM DONOR??!! I want our kids to be ours! To have a chance of
getting Patrick's ginger hair and social charms! He'll veto a sperm
donor, for sure.

Ican'tbreatheIcan'tcallhimIcan'tbearthis.

All my hopes and dreams. No wonder we couldn't fucking get pregnant. I love him! I can't leave him! I want his babies! This isn't fair! Why is this happening to us?

I flee to my bedroom and in a moment my pillow is soaked.
This bed is the only safe space for me right now.
I don't move from it. I can't.

Doctor Baby-Maker

His lairy shirt calls us in from the waiting room.
It's not Hawaiian, but a pricey subversion –
all-over red tulips and gold-emerald hummingbirds.
Shiny green pointy shoes. We get it –
he's not afraid to break norms.
A broad smile, gets to the point.
How long we've been trying,
ages, sperm results –
FINE! Fine???? FINE!!!!
    (Who would have thought
    eighty percent abnormal sperm morphology was actually fine?!
    Thanks for nothing you treacherous bastard Doctor Fucking Google,
    all that wasted asphyxiating hysterics and despair!)
periods (fine),
my blood tests and egg stores (fine).
Diagnoses us with Unexplained Infertility (SO NOT FINE!!)
Recommends Ovulation Induction with Intrauterine Insemination
then if no luck with that, IVF.
Chance of success: about twenty-five percent
per embryo transfer for a woman my age.

My anxiety tumbles into action,
asks a stack of questions including how having a baby through IVF
might affect the short and long-term health and development
of the baby (it doesn't),
explain I'm not sure I want to meddle

in what should be a natural process.
He reminds me that I'm only getting older
and each year the chances lessen.

Look, he says, turning his palms to the sky
and offering a well-rehearsed smile of reassurance –
a baby is a baby.
I can guarantee you that not one parent
who ends up with a real live baby in their arms,
gazing into its eyes,
ever gives a second thought as to how that baby was made.

If you want a baby,
stick with me
and I'm confident
I can make you a baby.

Lining up for the drop tower

For some reason we don't need long to deliberate.
In the kitchen when we get home and make ourselves a cuppa
I expect an argument
but Patrick is a rational man –
the science and the stats are solid enough to sway him.
Twenty-five per cent per cycle – not bad odds.
Anyway he's not the one who'll cop the needles,
the probes, the blood tests, the operations.
He'll be able to do his not-so-invasive bit
in the privacy of a closed room.
He tells me he'll go along with it, if it's what I want to do.

I never thought I would take these next steps.
I believed I would let nature decide if we'd have a baby or not.
But now the compulsion overrides
everything else.

It feels like we've paid to get into the fair,
found the first ride to be a disappointment
– a lousy dodgem car ride where the cars go too slow –
so it's only natural we try the next one –
the drop tower,
and if that doesn't do it for us,
we're up for the roller-coaster.

New hope

It's funny what a relief it is
to lose hope in natural conception
while falling back and landing
awkwardly   but landing nonetheless
on a new hope –
hormone injections,
stimulated follicles,
ultrasounds,
egg harvests,
clean, spinning sperm
and the magic that might,
just might
          happen
in clear plastic petri dishes.

View

I roll up to the clinic via the ancient lift where the floor numbers
light up wrong.
In spite of that I'm tentatively positive.

There are lots of women about my age, or a bit older,
sitting around. Some with partners. All shapes and sizes.

We sit on sophisticated brown leather sofa chairs
with our blue disposable booties on,
bare legs goose-bumping in the aircon,
busy with smartphones – emails and Facebook.
We avoid each other's eyes.

I look out the window,
appreciate the distant aqua ocean,
think
at least we have a good view.

So nice

to finally be getting help from someone —
real help involving drugs, scans, injections
and a pap-smear-like insemination.

Off to the shop straight after

like it's normal

to have a friendly man in floral shirt, denim jeans
and blue disposable booties
squirt your partner's semen into your cervix
before Tuesday's veggie-box packing session.

Prohibited territory

Reading the newspaper,
feeling a bit queasy.
Could be the drugs, could be anything.

Mind slides into prohibited territory —
what if I AM pregnant?
How good would that be?
First Intrauterine Insemination (IUI) cycle!

Flutters in my stomach remembering
the tight waltz-hold of Bitter Disappointment —
rational mind steps in and scolds   *Enough!*

Five days till I can take the test ...

Focus!
On the article,
on one day at a time.

The future, the test,
everything that is to be
will come soon enough, as Patrick might matter-of-factly remind me.

Impossible, this Que Sera Sera dance.

What are all these medications doing to me?

Must not leap into the arms of Dr Google again

Experts and novices

All hope is now in the hands of the experts.
Give me a baby, we ask, opening our wallets.

We try on some new roles —
he, an untrained nurse —
  breaking
  glass
  vials,
  drawing
  up
  needles,

injecting me on the couch
while I gasp
and groan
(never a fan of needles).

    We have our own yellow sharps container
    which we hide
    when we're expecting guests.

  I try not to be an impatient patient.

Church opposition

Many times
I've thought about calling mum and dad
        to tell them what we're doing.

They know we've been failing to get pregnant,
that I've been slow-dancing with Misery.

I visit them on the weekend
in their flash surfside apartment in Caloundra.
Over a cuppa mum shows me a half-made blanket
of the softest white wool, bordered in apricot and lemon.
Do you like the blanket I'm knitting for your sister's baby?
I disintegrate   tears splosh into tea.

But they are Catholics
who go to church every Sunday,
believe in Papal proclamations.
Mum has a photo of the Virgin Mother on her bedside table,
        facing the view.

They would not be the supportive parents
I need them to be
if I tell them
we're ignoring 'God's plan'
and doing IVF.

Isolating

I can't talk to my friends with kids just now. Even thinking about them makes me want to cry. They didn't have any trouble conceiving. They try to understand but they can't. My explanations are interrupted by small hands tugging at their legs or the need to referee toy disputes as they attempt to offer 'how-to-get-pregnant' tips. Most of them don't contact me. I don't contact them. They probably don't have time in between shopping for nappies and calling the breastfeeding helpline.

Online fertility forums

There's a whole other world out there
most don't know about.
Another language not taught in schools.
It's only by immersing myself
in the world of DHs, IUIs and flashing signatures
that I begin to learn.
Desperation guides me in.

At first I am bewildered by posts like:
Thank-you everyone! I broke and took a test and it was BFN
but it's not over til AF sings and I'm not gonna give up hope until I see AF …
so if no sign of the witch I'll test again and hopefully get my BFP.

I google:
DH (Dear Husband),
IUI (Intrauterine Insemination),
BFN (Big Fat Negative),
AF (Aunt Flo; Menstruation),
FS (Fertility Specialist),
BT (Blood Test).

BFP is the one
we all strive for,
long for:
        the Big Fat Positive.

Pineapple planting

I encounter some great, evidence-based advice like:

OzGirl: *So I was wondering if anyone had any suggestions to improve my chances for a BFP!* ...

BeachBabyPlease: *I've heard pineapple core helps implantation. Have your man keep his boys cool (don't put computer on his lap, etc.)* ...

RedFrog: *I heard that pineapple has something in it that helps with implantation. The week after my IUI, I ate three pineapples and ended up pregnant (we are 12 weeks now). Don't know if it helped, but it was the most pineapple I ever ate :)*

OzGirl: *Sending hubby to the store today to stock up on pineapples!!! Couldn't hurt right?!*

Stepping in

My first post.
How much to reveal?
I have already spied a friend's ex in here.
I go undercover – MagicHappens33.
Will I find support in this online world of angst?

Need to avoid TMI (Too Much Information) –
some women tell everything,
list their entire fertility history, step-by-step,
in their signature below every post.

Can I feel at home in this world of flashing emoticons,
tragic stories and obsessional determination?

I write a paragraph, introduce my situation.
Vent about how hard it's been,
detail current meds,
ask if anyone else started with IUI cycles.

Within an hour I've received five replies.
Moonshine5 writes *Welcome hon!*
I know what you mean, it's so tough, isn't it? Friends don't understand.
My FS got me doing IUI as well. Was worth a shot but didn't work for us.
More *welcomes* and cheery *good lucks* from others.

In this online ether
I discover a safe place
to ask questions about drug doses,
compare details of transfer protocols,
whinge about the clinic nurse who doesn't call back,
share disappointments, anxieties, heartbreak.

All anonymous.

The emotional posts of the infertile
are treated with tenderness,
      (not a lot of that around lately)
a solidarity born from experience.

I'm glad I stepped into this room.

Needle advice

Today I finish my update: *By the way, I am taking Pregnyl for luteal phase support (as my luteal phase in a natural cycle can be a bit short sometimes), and I find them to be the worst needles — so thick and blunt! Usually my partner gives them to me but I have to do the 3rd one myself this Thursday as he's away — not looking forward to it — I'm the sort of person who has to look away when having my blood taken — I hate needles! Any tips on technique — slow and steady or a sudden jab?!*

Moonshine5 responds: *Re the Pregynl needle, they sound similar to Clexane which causes massive bruising. I find the best approach to be as slow as you can be with inserting and also injecting. Good luck.*

KT82 suggests: *With needles a lot of ladies put a disinfected 50 cent coin in the freezer and put that on the skin on the jab site. I found that helps heaps. I, like you, hate BTs and needles but as DH leaves at 5AM to get on the tractor and is not in the door again til 9PM then it is me or no-one.*

I try the frozen fifty cent piece tip.
I find it really helps.
Thanks KT82.

Best friends

I don't know much about them
except how many embryos they got last cycle
and how long they've been trying,
but Moonshine5 and KT82 have become my best friends
in the land of the empty pram.

Opening up

I have only felt the need to confess
face-to-face with a stranger
twice:

once during a business management course,
when an exercise in pairs
on employee health issues
tipped me into disclosure

and the second time
while being monitored for side-effects by a nurse
after jabbing me with the flu vax
and the whole needle experience led me to reflect aloud.

Both times, it turned out,
each of them had been through IVF too.

Grief and bleaching

At home on my birthday
I grieve.

Bitter
about our bodies' failures,
the lack of a 'desired outcome'.

Those who 'achieve'
natural conception
have no idea what a gift it is.

The months plod past,
birthday after birthday ticks by,
coral reefs bleach irreparably

I keep wondering

how much time do we have, really?

Things that make me happy

A bear hug from behind,
watching Gotye sing at the Seafront Oval
as twilight flying-foxes jet high above us.

Running the length of the Esplanade at dawn
to the riotous racket of rainbow lorikeets,
the sun waking up the sleepy waters of the bay.

A new employee serving
our regulars with gusto and charm,
refilling canisters without being asked.

A veggie feast with friends,
comparing run times and basketball scores,
laughter over Pictionary and Killer Bunnies.

Sliding into fresh bamboo sheets,
resting my weariness on a memory-foam pillow,
warming my hands on Patrick's skin.

Ignoring to-do lists,
putting my phone on airplane mode
and hammocking the whole day away.

Floating above a flourishing reef,
letting the shallow water dance me,
watching luminous rock-cods chomp purple coral.

Mint and lemon iced soda-water,
succulent mangoes, ripe lychees fresh off the tree —
the taste of summer, sweet in my mouth.

The voice of my best friend, Holly,
thousands of kilometres away,
cheerily offering me the use of her womb.

Test

Today I did the pregnancy test as scheduled.
I didn't do it a week before
or even a day before, like some eager women do.
I waited until they told me to.
I was in no hurry to get out of bed and do it.

I've been here too many times –
waiting for the second blue line that never appears.

I knew it was too much to hope
that my slightly aching breasts were due to a successful cycle.
I knew it was too much to believe
that the slight stomach cramps
these last couple of days were due to conception
rather than side-effects of the injections.

I don't even have signs of PMT yet
but this negative result I am holding
heralds their imminent arrival

like guests you can't say no to
when they invite themselves to your party.

Bloody period

Lottery

It's a hard slog to get through work today.
I feel like screaming when I have to steam mop the floor
after a kid playing with the bulk olive oil tap
let a litre or two dribble and spread across the floor
in a slippery celebration of failure.

I distract myself at times by thinking about
what I would do if I won Lotto –
there's a seventy-million-dollar draw tonight.
I don't even have a ticket.
Maybe I should get one –
it might be easier to win Lotto
                    than to get pregnant.
I wish I could indulge in a bottle of wine and a movie,
but life goes on,
I've got too much to do.

On the way home, I think better of it and call in to my local shops.
Now to deal with Crushing Disappointment Number Thirty-Eight
I'm armed
with Red Rock Deli salt and vinegar chips,
Bridesmaids DVD,
Golden Gaytime ice-cream,
bottle of Four Sisters Merlot

and a Lotto QuickPick.

Opposites

We are opposites — we attract.
Yet our eggs and sperm can't get together.
Is nature trying to tell us something?

Critical decade

Climate change really worries me.
I've heard the scientists' warnings of what Earth will be like
in twenty, fifty, eighty years.

I want to have children now
so they can enjoy living on a planet
where giraffes still roam wild,
not existing only as squeaky toys.

If we have kids, I want to be able to show them
the truly Great Barrier Reef before it's gone.
This is the critical decade.

The longer this fertility debacle goes on, the more I wonder —
is the universe trying to save me
for the campaign work that needs doing now?

How much of an activist can I be
as a mother of young children?
But I could still be involved,
raise them well
so they can help in the looming struggles
to protect our precious planet, couldn't I?

We just want what so many want —
a family of our own.

Waiting

Now, instead of waiting for a positive pregnancy test,
I'm waiting for my period to come.

Just want it to arrive with its bold   *Hello, I'm here!*
instead of knocking loudly,
laying cramps at the doorstep
and running away.

Skimming across the surface

Patrick and I head to the beach after work —
he for a kite-surf, me for a simple swim.

Wind whips sand into our legs and faces.

We love opposite conditions, of course.

Wind exhilarates him, kite soaring higher,
skimming him across the choppy surface.
I just want a peaceful swim in the sedate salty bay.

I complain about the wind but he ignores me,
spreading out gear and clipping on his harness.

I stretch my cap and goggles over my head,
lunge in and swim freestyle towards the horizon for as long as I can.

Endurance is becoming my forte.

Invisible undercurrent

Infertility
or sub-fertility
or just fucking stubborn fertility —
the invisible undercurrent
beneath our lives.

A private process.
A painful striving
that only we know about.

The fulcrum
on which any decision rests.
The winner of all calendar conflicts.

Only we share its details,
the constant imminence of tears,
the insertion of needles into tired skin,
the daily counting and measuring and mating to order.

It's a glue that binds us now,
but we know

it could crack us apart.

For sale

My best friend posts a picture
of the pram she's selling
on Facebook.

I can't help myself –
I click on it.

Looks comfortable,
toddler seat and all.
A one-hundred-and-fifty-dollar bargain.

I want to type   *I'll take it.*

For the two children
I should have had by now.

Drifting in the wind

Day off.   Sick?
Not really.   Headachy, morose, lethargic, utterly unable to smile …

Simply cannot pack my bag with tampons (again) and face work.

Lying on the couch,
my toes wiggle in the sunshine streaming through the window.

Low grey clouds float and morph in patches across the sky.

Brilliant red flowers from my neighbour's flame tree
drift in the wind like confetti.

Raindrops glint, catching the confused sun,
falling in gusty diagonals.

Gum trees rustle in bursts of breezy excitement.
Frangipanni fragrance infuses the air.

I talk to my sister on the phone,
am reminded   we all have our troubles.

Smile formation

At the end of every day,
a needle.

Before bed —
the routine jabbing, stabbing.

It seems like half a year of needles
but it's only been two months.
Seventeen per month.

Secret red pinpricks decorate
my belly, below my navel,
in a smile formation.

This is where a little extra fat is an advantage.
An indisputable excuse for Burger Rings.

Accomplishment

Normally I get Patrick to do it
but tonight the drive to be independent
momentarily overcomes my needle phobia.

I position the point of the needle against my soft skin.
Using the gentlest pressure,
it slowly sinks in, almost before I realise.

I am surprised   *I can do this!*

After finishing the procedure,
I cap the needle-pen, put it back in the box,
put the box back in the fridge
behind the beers on the bottom shelf
and smile at Patrick proudly.

I did it!

He celebrates with me.

After a few nights, I realise I must have hit a lucky spot —
they're not all that easy and pain-free —
but I continue on
becoming

self-injector extraordinaire.

Text only

Lying on our coffee table
even the front cover of the air-conditioner manual
sports a photo of a mother looking down and smiling
lovingly into her baby's eyes.

I flip it over
so the back cover
faces up,

text only.

Broken-down escalator

We didn't have a wedding —
I was too feminist for that.
But we were hoping to have a baby.

Patrick's fortieth is coming up,
so we decide to throw a big party,
god knows we need to liven things up.

As we hit the phones to tell people to save the date,
it becomes clear
that pregnant family and friends

with different due dates,
in different states,
can't travel that close to his birthday.

Suddenly even our party plans
grind to a halt,
our enthusiasm seizes up,

and in its place
the sense of standing still
on a broken-down escalator

watching everyone else rising up in a fully-functioning lift.

Open

I undress while Dr Baby-Maker goes to the lab to collect the sperm.
I place my feet on the footplates at the end of the gurney,
lean back, spread my legs.

He returns, asks for names, birth dates.
I rattle off mine, Patrick's.
He lifts the sheet,
inserts a clamp to keep my vagina open,
peers, prods inside.

You're not usually difficult, are you?
frowning at my uncooperative cervix.
Ok, open now, he directs it.

My insides feel invaded.
I feel the tube going in,
slight pain, pressure.
There, done, he says cheerily.

I'm due to come back this afternoon for an appointment
to discuss IVF, the next stage,
if this Intrauterine Insemination Take Three is all a waste of time.

You're spending most of the day here, aren't you?
he murmurs sympathetically.
Yes, I say, pulling my jeans on behind the curtain.

This time was more uncomfortable than the first two.
Perhaps the situation is hitting home.
Although I consented to this,
I'm feeling undignified and violated.

I am suddenly sorry for myself, fragile.
I grab a tissue, tears fall, I can't help it.
I make a quick exit, don't look at him as I squeeze out *Thanks, bye,*
head for the lift, wait forever for its archaic doors to slowly roll
open.
Thank god it's empty.
Sobbing loudly now,
I will it not to open for anyone on the way down.

I can't stop thinking —
        This is not how I wanted to make a baby.

Endless possibilities

On Sunday arvo I head out
to meet Sylvia and her two girls at Planet 72.
The girls squeal and literally jump up and down
in front of the seventy-two flavours on offer.

I choose a scoop of mango sorbet
with a half-scoop of macadamia on top.
The girls change their minds twenty times
before, ice-creams already melting,
we make our way over the zebra crossing
to sit and lick at a picnic table in the shade
beside the Esplanade walking track.

You're not looking too flash, you know, Jade,
Sylvia comments tentatively, concern showing
above her boysenberry in a waffle cone.

I know you've put so much effort in,
and done all the right things,
and don't take this the wrong way,
but have you thought it might be better for you
(and Patrick),
if you call it quits,
focus on something else?

She stops to grab an extra serviette from her bag,
wipes her youngest daughter's face
before the ice-cream drips from her chin onto her red romper.

You've got so much to offer the world, you know.
Plenty of people can be mums,
but not many could have opened Ripe
and built it up so it's the go-to place
for everyone in this town who cares about the planet.
You could expand,
build your own chain,
write a book,
do guest lectures on sustainability at schools —
the possibilities are endless!

I don't trust myself to respond.
Focus on my ice-cream.
So she goes on, voice a little shaky.

You know you can play more of a role in my kids' lives if you like.
You're already Aunty Jade, but you can do more, be more, if you want.
The kids love you.

Thanks Sylv, but you know, nothing's the same as having a kid of your own.

My gaze blurs and pixelates at the sight of a pair of mums
jogging and chatting while they push
fancy big-wheeled prams along the path.

Yeah, I get that. And I'm here for you if you want to keep going.
I'm just concerned about what it's doing to you.
You haven't been out with me and the others for ages,
you don't visit like you used to.
You just don't seem to smile much anymore...
you always seem tense, withdrawn.
Is it really worth it?

She looks so compassionate
but her words chill me,
more than ice-cream,
more than if hailstones were pelting
down my back.

You're right, I'm not coping too well right now,
It'll get better ...   Deep sigh.
The Doctor thinks we're good candidates for IVF.
I ... I just have to find the energy for the next step.

I take big bites of my cone, finishing it off swiftly,
make excuses and head home.

Patrick's out playing basketball
and doesn't notice (or doesn't care to notice?)
my flushed, tear-stained face
when he returns
and disappears straight into the shower.

I don't want to talk to him about it anyway.

What if he agrees with Sylvia?

Bloody period

Pancake therapy

Thank god. Misty can fill in for Evie.
That's the staffing sorted for the market stall.

I'm a dancer who's forgotten
    all the moves,
        can't even hear the music.

I force myself to do what I know helps.
Ride down to the Esplanade,
nab a beanbag under a coconut palm.
At Enzo's I order
banana and syrup pancakes, a chai latte.
The Saturday cyclists roll up in their fluoro lycra,
crowd around the tall tables with views.

The tide is out, miles out.
Light plays on the moist dips and rivulets
in the golden-beige sand.
After I finish my sickly-sweet breakfast
I walk along the beach, trying not to scowl
at all the fellow walkers who chirp *Hi!* as they pass.

I wish they would ignore me.
The last thing I feel like doing is
smiling,
greeting,
pretending
    everything
        is okay.

Willing the sand to swallow me

It's not okay.
I can't do this.

I collapse   sapped.
Bend my knees up and wrap my arms around them,
willing the sand to open up and swallow me.

I'm a complete failure.
I'm never going to be a mother.
This damn quest. It's going to be my downfall.
Sylvia's right. I'm depressed.
Soon I'm not going to be able to get up in the morning,
let alone run a business.
Ripe is making good profits, but not enough
to pay for IVF and cover a replacement manager
for an extended period if I go to pieces.
I'll have to sell the business.

I stay there for an hour or more, closed,
        a tight ball of despair.
As the morning wears on
a small speck of self-preservation nudges me
to move before I get really sunburnt.
Like a pathetic damsel-in-distress I call Patrick,
bawl into the phone, shakily
ask him to come to collect me, my misery, and my bike.

He's shooting baskets with a friend
but he comes.

When he's brought me safely home,
he sits beside me on the couch, extends his arm
heavily across my shoulders.

We can stop.
If it's too much.

I don't want to stop!   I howl.

Okay.   Okay.

But he looks fierce,
heads out to the shed
to do   who knows what?

Accelerating

But maybe I do want to stop? I can't go on like this can't sleep got maybe two hours last night even a new mother would get more than that I think about getting up getting dressed sliding into my green Barina accelerating towards Maryborough reaching the stretch where you can go over one hundred clicks veering off the road slamming into the first big tree I just can't see the point anymore.

But   I won't.   I mustn't.

I couldn't do that to Patrick, to my family.

At midday, ignoring the insistence of my phone,
I get up and force myself
to eat some muesli and berries.
With food on board, I become slightly more rational.

I need to stop this.

Give up trying to make a baby.

I'm just not up to doing IVF.

I need to rescue my relationship while there's still a chance.

Shit.   I don't know what to do.

Wise counsel

I call the clinic,
      book in to see their counsellor.
She's an older woman,
      short grey hair, glasses.
She listens, asks questions, helps me balance pros and cons,
      work out what I want.
She validates
      how hard it has been.
She encourages open communication
      with Patrick.
Helps me develop a self-care plan,
      a crisis plan.
It includes a week off work.
      I can arrange that, I'm the boss, I will.
It includes planning quality time with Patrick.
      Sure, I can try that,
      it's not like I'm already the only one
      planning everything else to do with 'us',
      but yeah, I can add this to my to-do list.
She instils confidence, hope.
      Reminds me of all I have done.
Reassures me of the process,
      the support available,
the potential joyful outcome
      that could make this whole saga worthwhile.
I can do this.
      We can do this.
         We will.

3.

Bring on the roller-coaster

Crying
while listening to the nurse go through her book of diagrams,
carefully explaining all the stages and procedures
like I'm a bit slow on the uptake –

I can't decide if
IVF has come
too soon or
not soon enough.

Magic spot

Check it out! Grace joins the guys
back with their catch.
SO many whiting!
You must have found a magic spot!

Amy and I stroll over to inspect the haul
along with a small posse of sun-kissed kids.
Not bad at all! I say flatly,
not excited about a fresh-fish dinner.
The kids count the lithe silver bodies,
Patrick and his mates begin to scale and fillet.

Well, now we can kick back with a drink
while the boys do dinner! Grace proclaims,
setting out cheese and crackers on the fold-out table
in the shaded centre of the campsite.
Shall I crack open the sav blanc I bought? I ask,
lolling in my gum-tree-slung hammock.
Sure, let me grab it for you, is it in this esky? Grace asks,
        heading towards it.
Oh, it's okay, I can get it!
I spring awkwardly out of the hammock,
dash to the esky
and manoeuvre the bottle out from between
        milk, juice, and a pack of syringes.

Later we sit in a circle under the stars,
campfire crackling.
We chat, pass salty chips,
ignore kids resisting sleep in their tents.
I catch Patrick's eyes and nod in the direction of our tent.
We both rise quietly.
I grab the medication from the esky,
he delves into the bag for a head-torch.

In the tent we hope our friends don't notice
our needle-jabbing shadows.
He injects me slowly   I suppress a cry of pain.
I rummage for the bright yellow sharps container,
stick the spent needle in.

We go back out,
slide the box of syringes into the esky
in the dim light of the fire,
try to join the conversation
about kids who won't eat fruit.

Responding too well

Twenty one follicles!
Twelve on one side, nine on the other.
Lying awkwardly on the bench,
I write the length of each one on a clipboard
as Dr Baby-Maker manoeuvres his large wand
slowly around inside me,
measures the follicles on his screen
and gets me to record their stats.

These fuzzy black oval shapes are my follicles.
Usually only one,
now there are twenty-one.
I'm responding well to the medication,
maybe too well.
The risk now is Ovarian Hyper-Stimulation Syndrome (OHSS).

No wonder
I am tired,
bloated,
uncomfortable,
nauseous.

They tell me we may need to wait after fertilizing the eggs —
they may all need to be frozen,
and it'll be another month at least
before an embryo can be put in —
my ovaries will need time to recover.

Another episode in this fertility saga.

Why did I expect things to go to plan?

Risk

Now, on top of feeling tired, nauseous and uncomfortable,
    I'm scared.

Researching Hyper-Stimulation
I obsess about what could happen if I get a clot.
Just two days ago, I happened to read
about how taking the pill caused such high oestrogen levels
in a young medical student that she developed a clot.
It broke free and blocked blood vessels in her brain
causing her to have a stroke.
She died.

The advice on OHSS includes conflicting messages.
Women are told to keep legs active to decrease the risk of clots
as well as being warned against exercising too strenuously
as that could further damage swollen ovaries.

I'm scared.
What have we done –

      opening the door to danger,
      to high-tech medicine –
      in our haste,
      our quest

      to get to first base.

Hyperstimulation

Lying in bed at night,
my abdomen takes over.

Heavy, bloated, active,
the follicles jostle for space.

My ovaries and my mind —
hyper-stimulated.

I'm short of breath —
is that just anxiety
       or a telling indicator of something dire?

The doctors have conned me.
I've become their laboratory,
a follicle-production-factory.

There are twenty-one of the damn things,
putting my life,   my LIFE!
at risk.

I never asked for that many.
It's unnatural,
feels unnatural.

Three more distended days till they can be drained.

And they say the riskiest time for OHSS is *after* egg collection.

What kind of life-threatening turmoil
will their medical experiment throw me into then?

My body's balance is in chaos —
my kidneys, liver and lungs could all be harmed,
I could have a stroke ...

I should have updated my will.

Too many

Even simple walking leads to stitches.
I make an effort to go out with friends.

I sit in the restaurant conscious of the movement inside me.
Like a pregnant woman
      but not.

Instead of one natural embryo growing
I have twenty-one turbo-charged eggs!

So much for clearly specifying
I didn't want too many.

Intimacy

Tonight tears slide down my cheeks
      as Patrick injects the second needle.
I grip his shoulder
as he focuses on depressing the syringe slowly
into my bruised belly flesh.

I hate injecting you   he's upset
that our intimate moments have become   this.

The feeling's mutual, I joke
although I am grateful
he can plunge me with the thicker, blunter needle
because I can only do the first, thinner one,
the one that slides in almost of its own accord,
with the tenderest of pressure.

I can't bring myself
to force the thick needle through my skin,
through the loyal layers
that try
to defend

my body's fast-dwindling integrity.

Overstimulation

Another scan.
Twenty-eight follicles this time.
Excess fluid.
Almost certain to develop OHSS,
may need hospitalization.

Four days (at least) away from the shop.
I call Evie,
explain what needs doing to cover me,
instruct her to tell the others I have the flu.

The doctor has given me a softer triggering drug,
a nasal spray this time.
At least we've seen the last of injections for a while.

And I'm told I'll have to wait
(god, I'm so sick of waiting)
two whole cycles before an embryo can be put in.

I cry as the nurse explains it all to me.

It's likely that seventy percent of the eggs will be retrieved.
If all fertilize
(and I don't know what the probability of that is)
we'll potentially have twenty embryos. Twenty.

Then there's approximately a twenty-five percent success rate.
How many embryonic lives will be discarded?

This is not what I wanted.

A different doctor today.
Says I have polycystic-looking ovaries
but not the polycystic ovarian syndrome that affects fertility.
Wouldn't explain further when I questioned him.
It had never been mentioned before,
at any of the previous scans.
I really need to know more.
He brushes me aside   *nothing to worry about.*

I miss my regular doctor.
He would have explained things.
Why did he have to take a Hawaiian holiday right now?

And, I'm told, I'll have a third, unknown doctor
for my egg retrieval op in two days' time.

At home I rock in the hammock on our back deck,
shaded by my favourite old gum-tree,
listen to the magpies.

Getting creative with medicine

Haven't these people heard of tablets?
Noooo … that would be a far too easy,
way too *normal*
a way to take medication.

No, now it's three types of needles and a nasal spray —
four sprays every fifteen minutes
          over the course of an hour
                    into alternating nostrils.

Every time   the sudden irritation
causes my eyes to clench tight,
my nose to redden and sting.

The second part of the cycle,
when we do eventually get to that,
involves a progesterone pessary
          into the vagina
                    twice a day.

Creativity abounds   it seems
when devising methods to medicate a body
enduring IVF.

Oh   to simply swallow a pill.

Grand total

The grand total is   I am told
as I'm waking up from the anaesthetic:
thirty-seven eggs.

I get them to repeat it a few times,
I must be hearing wrong.

The nurse quips   *You're a bit of an overachiever*

and through the fogginess and disbelief,
I smile
       because generally-speaking, I am.

Post-op

I rub my nose repeatedly
and cry compulsively
(common urges after a general, the nurse explains).

Pain grips my abdomen, taking over.
They gradually add more analgesia into my cannula.
I have to rate my pain on a scale of one to ten, again and again.

Soon the medication kicks in,
my pain drops to a two or three
and I'm wheeled back to the ward.
A kind nurse brings me heat-packs, water, tomato sandwiches.

In a small room with a plastic seat, a sink and some porn magazines,
Patrick does the deed.

He says it was a walk of shame
passing all the knowing nurses in their station.

I reassure him
there isn't anything shameful about it,
tell him   *well done.*

Now we have both played our part.
We can sit back, relax,
wait for the results of our efforts,
keeping all fingers crossed.

After lunch, although I'm scared to go home,
I face the inevitable and shuffle out,
under strict instructions to drink water,
take the meds,
weigh myself daily
and present to Emergency if I feel too sick.

Drugs, drugs and more drugs

I'm about to throw up in the chemist
waiting for them to fill my scripts.
Patrick has to agitate for them to give me a plastic bag
and I sit there, dizzy and nauseous,
while they explain to him their reasons
for not giving us all the medications on the script.

We eventually walk out with stuff
for inflammation, mild pain, serious pain,
nausea, constipation, indigestion,
blood clot prevention and pelvic fluid retention.

Lucky I have a list
telling me what to take and when.

Not feeling too smurfy

Two days of constipation.
One sachet of Movocol, one pear and a glass of prune juice
tip me over into diarrhoea and hours of stomach pain
on top of my already painful, swollen ovaries.

A Smurfs movie keeps me entertained for a while,
bringing back childhood memories
of Smurfette, Gargamel and Brainy.

Football team

Twenty-seven.
That's how many eggs have successfully fertilised.

I hang up the phone and text Patrick.
We joke about
having enough to start our own cult, football team,
or revolutionary youth brigade.

Really, we are in shock,
and I start to worry about the ethical dilemmas
of potentially having leftover frozen embryos.

I do not want to have to make those decisions.

I go online,
trawl through blogs and forums
to read about other peoples' bounties –
can't find anyone reporting as many as ours,
and so many end up
with very few eggs and embryos
to show for their discomfort,
then have to go through it all –
the needles, surgery and risks –
again and again.

I guess in this case, for us,
if it doesn't rain
       it bloody pours.

Breaking the news

I call Mum and Dad on Facetime tonight,
break the news about us trying IVF.

Oh   mum murmurs.
Dad's heavy forehead creases.
Doesn't say another word,
stares at a spot on the wall to my left.

Mum asks a few questions about what's involved.
I keep my answers vague.

I know you really want a baby
        but I didn't think you would do IVF, she finally says,
                clasping her hands tightly in front of her.

Yeah, well neither did we. But we think it's worth a try.

She switches to a brighter pitch   *And how's the shop going?*

Irises and daisies

Day two post-egg-pick-up.
Home alone,
feeling tired, restless, bloated (still),
sorry for myself.

I scull copious glasses of water
even though it adds to the nausea.
It's really hard to do everything I'm told,
especially drink three litres of water a day.

I hear someone come down the path onto our deck.
No knock.
I peer through the spy-hole and see someone
placing something carefully on the table,
a dash of colour.

My heart lifts — has someone sent me flowers?
I open the door and go out.
A gorgeous arrangement
of carnations, irises and daisies.

There's a fluttering note —
> *Just a small bunch of flowers*
> *to wish you well and let you know we're thinking of you*
> *and wishing you success. Mum and Dad xo*

I begin to bawl before I even make it back inside.

I'm touched that they care more for me
than the Pope's edicts,

that they think what I'm going through

deserves flowers.

Progress report

I call the clinic.   Twenty-seven.
That's how many fertilised eggs have developed
into two-day old embryos.
ALL of them.
Holy moly.

Twenty-seven little embryonic people-to-be
with one-hundred percent our genes.
Not sure if I want to shout for joy, cry, or both at once.

If one in four cycles ends up in a pregnancy,
we only need eight to have two children, statistically.
That's nineteen *leftovers*.
And we may be lucky and only need two.

That'd mean even more   *leftovers.*
What a terrible term to use for a potential person.

Of course, it depends on so many variables,
how well they thaw out,
and we might go through them all
if we're unlucky with implantation
or growing them to full-term.

So many couples would give anything
to be given that kind of news from the clinic.
I guess we should err on the side of celebration.

Our eggs and sperm do like each other after all.

I would crack open some champers,
splurge on some chocolates,
but I'm still feeling ghastly.
The nurse said I was sounding good
when I answered questions about my weight, my wee, my pain,
but she warned that the worst could still be on its way,
the five-day-post-egg-pick-up being the real danger time.

I resist the urge to call my parents and tell them the news,
certain that our twenty-seven embryos would shock
traditional right-to-lifers.

Question

Will these minute,
four-cell munchkins
like my womb
as much as they like
their petri dish?

Next steps

They all go in the freezer.
Twenty-seven *frosties*
waiting for my cycle to settle.
Ovaries still bruised, recovering slowly.
Internal scans make me late for work,
leave me completely lacking in desire
and feeling vulnerable
(enduring a long, condom-covered probe
investigating your intimate internals twice a week
will do that to a woman).

Patrick and I talk about where we are at,
our diminished sex life.
He's distanced from the process now.
You don't even need me anymore. Unless they're a dud batch.

It's just me
        my cycles,
        my scans,
        my urine tests,
        my blood tests

and the *frosties*
that we
(with help)
have made.

Next step: the doctor will place
one each month
into me with a plastic tube.

You can give me the needles, if you like
        I suggest   with a dry smile.

The lesson of the lift

The lift to the IVF clinic tries to teach me patience.

After I press the button three times quickly,
(a trick I learnt from someone else)
the doors finally ease shut.

It's hard to tell if we are moving.
It is so slow.
Motionless, almost,
like we aren't going anywhere.

 Finally, we make it
          to the second floor.

Transfer

On the screen
for a moment
they flash up an image of our three-celled embryo.
At two-days-old it was four cells
but after thawing, it lost two
then started growing.
We're all hoping it will continue
to grow inside my eager womb.

It's a quick procedure,
transferring it through a tube into my uterus,
and before we know it
we're in the lift on the way down.
The rest of the day I lie around, watching movies,
resting up so that I don't unsettle the little one inside me.

Am I technically pregnant now?
It's impossible for people who conceive naturally
to know if they are pregnant with a two-day old embryo
so I have special knowledge.
Is it better not to know?

If it doesn't stick,
I will be mourning the loss of a potential baby
when non-IVF couples would be blissfully unaware
that it had even been there,
briefly residing,
in warm, blood-rich tissue,
full of promise.

My whole attitude towards friends with babies
has turned a corner.
Now that we have embryos in the freezer
I feel positive,
like it's only a matter of time,
embryos plus experts *has* to equal babies,
sooner or later,
doesn't it?

Not so much Facebook envy

These days I don't feel that soft stab of envy
every time I see cute baby photos on Facebook.

Or disgruntled about having to always go to friends' homes for dinner
so their kids can be put to bed in their own cots.

Instead I feel the tentative camaraderie
of someone who has filled in all the right forms
and is merely waiting to join the club.

Motives

Every now and again
my mind drifts to the image of the embryo
they flashed up on the screen.

Only three cells.
Four, when they got it out of the freezer, they said.
I know there were plenty of six-celled ones in the batch,
           even a seven.
Why didn't they choose one of them?
Is it because that would improve the chances
and we wouldn't need to come back?
How much money does the clinic make
for every embryo transfer?

I wish our public health system offered fertility services —
then I could be sure
there was no profit motive directing the moves.

I saw Dr Baby-Maker parking on the Esplanade
in his bright orange BMW convertible.

What's he really considering
           when he chooses which embryo to use?

So small

This Two Week Wait isn't so bad.
It's the wait after our first IVF implantation
and despite seeing our three-celled embryo up on the screen,
we've only allowed small hope to develop   not big hope.

I think hope works to a bell curve.
We're well past the middle stages of high hope,
big desperate expectations,
crushing disappointments.

We've learnt
there are unexplained barriers
to us getting pregnant
and it's best to believe
that this month
will be no different
to the forty-two months before.

I know not to think of that three-celled embryo
as our baby —
a period is bad enough,
let alone thinking of it
as a miscarriage.

So small,
if it wasn't for science,
we wouldn't have known about it
at all.

Thank god for bubbles

I'm an aunty again.
My new niece is gorgeous on Facebook,
exquisite face framed with thick dark hair.

On the same day
the red messenger delivers the news —
our first proper cycle has failed.

Other people give birth to babies.
I give birth to disappointment.   Again.
I also give birth to marketing plans,
performance development reviews
and shop newsletters.

Tonight we pop champagne
and drink.
Thank god for bubbles
lifting us into tipsiness.
With each sip,
loss temporarily loses its way,
dissolves.

I devour a box of Smarties for dinner.
Next morning
hurts
not just because of the headache.

I definitely need to wait a week or two
before venturing into the baby clothes department
to buy a gift for my niece.

Unexplained Infertility

What's really annoying
is that there's nothing wrong with us,
as far as they can tell.

You'd think that would be a good thing,
but when people find out we're doing IVF,
they assume we have problems with our sperm
or eggs
or tubes
or something.

I don't like people thinking we are somehow defective
when to the best of our knowledge we're not.
I feel like shouting   *there's nothing wrong with us!*

But of course that's not entirely true.
What's wrong with us
is that we really want to
        but can't
                get pregnant.

Burnt out

After the first failed cycle
people comfort us   *Oh, don't worry, it'll happen,*
they say it takes three or four tries before IVF works.

They don't have a clue —
the years of trying   and trying
all the cycles of hope and disappointment
that have come before this particular cycle.

The needles and tests and embryos that substitute
for fun   for a life.

I'm almost past caring now.
I don't even think I'll be excited
         if it ever does happen.
It's all too statistical.
The time for simple excitement was years ago.
We've had too long to think
         every gruelling step of the way ...
                  should we bother?
                           how much do we really want a child?

If you get pregnant relatively quickly,
you can't know what that's like,
the constant decision-making,
weighing up the pros and cons,

wondering how determined you should be,
how much medicine and technology you're prepared to try.
Each month, how much further should you go?

The arctic ice is melting fast, the world's going to shit.
Who ever thought it would be so fucking hard to get pregnant?
And if it ever happens
everyone will be beaming with joy,
expecting me to be over the moon,
but I'm utterly burnt

          out.

Joy will have a hard time sprouting amongst the scars.

For Christ's sake, I just want to get on with my life.

Treatment for a broken foot

Why don't you just adopt?   my brother asks,
incredulous that we would put ourselves through all this.
He's older than me and has three kids of his own, of course.

I give him a bleak beige answer
but I could ask

If you had a broken, infected foot,
wouldn't you want the doctor to help you
to fix it if they could?

If infertility can be treated,
shouldn't we try?

To a point

I feel so hopeless.
Nothing excites me.

I'm working back at the shop,
paying the week's invoices
when I realise I can't sit with it by myself anymore.

Call my friend Amy.
Haven't confided in her before.
I explain what's been happening
or not happening to be precise.
Pour my anguish down the grey plastic phone.

She's empathetic
              to a point.

> *Maybe you should slow down a bit, Jade.*
> *Your busy lifestyle, all that's involved in running a business,*
> *might not create the optimum conditions, you know.*
> *Stress and all that, might disrupt the natural process?*

You think I haven't endlessly thought about that?
Besides, plenty of people in super stressful jobs,
in domestic violence situations,
in war zones, for god's sake, they get pregnant! I snap.
And who's going to run the business for me?

Yeah, good points, it just seems like your body
might be trying to tell you something.

I politely finish the call.
Want to scream
at the stifling walls of my tiny office,
banal and useless
as her desk-calendar advice.

Sigh

Our second frozen embryo transfer.
I feel flat and grey,
sullen as this day of low dense cloud.

I should be happy – day off work,
another exciting chance to make a baby –

but I feel   well, I guess the best word for it is
        lonely.

Waiting at home,
I check through emails,
make a cup of tea,
fritter through the hours until
the appointment.
Think of my sister and various friends at home with their babies,
think of the years rolling by –
we just made plans for another Christmas.

It helps to meet Patrick at the clinic.
After paying the IVF invoices at reception,
we settle into the chairs with the best view.

I look out at the rooftops in the distance
and let out a big sigh.

Patrick pockets his mobile and reaches for my hand.

Hoping for a stayer

This time they flash it up on the screen
and, to me, it looks healthier,
cells clearly defined.
They explain the two others they chose before this one
didn't survive the thawing.

This one was four cells when frozen, just grown to six.
Hope germinates. Followed by more statistics.
We have about a thirty percent chance this month.

I head home, put my feet up,
allow a little hope to unfurl.
Maybe if I make up names for it
and send loving messages its way,
bond with it psychologically,
it will hang in there?

Or maybe that's a recipe for more pain,
more disappointment
and I should just get on with things,

ignore it
until it's ready to prove itself
a stayer.

I play with names anyway,
an hour (or two!) of researching,
making lists,
fantasizing —

having a bet each way.

Welcoming womb

Today
I yearn for sun.
Five minutes into my morning run
I'm bombarded with raindrops heavy as a fire hose.
I turn back, drenched, stamping in sudden puddles.

I didn't really have the energy for it anyway.

Today
I yearn for a welcoming womb
that can sustain this life we've placed inside it,
a womb that cushions and fiercely holds this life
rather than rejecting,
        ejecting it,
                into the sodden gloom.

Bloody period

Tally

I am annoyed at myself
for feeling this burnt out

after only
thirty-seven months of trying naturally
three Intra-Uterine Inseminations
two embryo transfers
twenty thousand litres of tears
two million tense moments with Patrick

and a heart that beats listlessly in my chest.

The poise of liquid nitrogen

I oscillate between
fateful nonchalance
        and painful yearning.

I think I'm handling it all fine,
then something jerks me
out of my admirable state of acceptance.

A news story about a child left tied to a Hills Hoist.

My sister casually mentioning how all the women in her mothers' group
have two children now
so it's hard to contain them all
in their homes for mothers' group,
        Such chaos, she laughs.

A pregnancy magazine on top of the pile in the hairdressers,
tempting me to pick it up,
flick through the bright maternity fashions
with a hidden self-pitying grimace.

I think about naming all twenty-five embryos
poised in the liquid nitrogen,
so if I never get to name a child,
at least I can experience naming the ones
that tease our lives with their four- or six-celled wholeness,
these children-to-be who may follow

their two slight siblings
by slipping through my lips
unnoticed.

But the idea exhausts me
before it's even half-formed.

Double protection

Spontaneous sex in the fertile window.
First time in years.

And poor Patrick's running around
searching for a condom.

It's two days before embryo transfer,
must avoid the possibility
of ending up with twins.

Years of paying for the pill,
taking the pill –
never realising
it was completely
        unnecessary for us.

And to think,
waiting for the 'right time' to start a family,
we frequently used condoms as well,
just in case …

Double protection for years.
What a joke.

Embryo away!

Will a baby come pushing through this new meltdown?
Can anything good ever emerge from the carnage
of my chosen, over-achieving life,
my urgent, society-changing ambitions?

My rest-defying schedule lies mangled around me.
Unable to get up to make dinner,
grounded by exhaustion.

I admit defeat – I can't do it all.
Can't face the shop,
the market stall,
organizing another damn thing.
Guilt, fear and irritation rampage like weeds.

My words become a waterfall of tears at the GP's.
She firmly prescribes a week off work to start with.
I feel shame.
Worry what my employees will think, how it will affect them.

I can't stand the ongoing judgement
of my brother and friends
who blame my infertility on my busy life.

The next day, furious at the crawling traffic, the decrepit lift,
I open my legs for Dr Baby-Maker.
Feeling lucky? he chirrups.

The white-coated lab assistant hovers beside him with her little tube.
Our first choice didn't survive the thaw
      but this one looks great!
Patrick massages my shoulder
as the four-celled life-form is pushed through the tube into my womb.

'*Embryo away!* The nurse says as she releases it',
smiles, wishes us luck and leaves the room.

After I've pulled on my jeans I open the curtain to face the doctor,
confess we aren't coping too well.

He urges us not to give up.

This is the hardest part of the journey, this IVF stage.
Let's hope it's third time lucky
and we can give you a positive pregnancy test to cheer you up.

All we can do is smile weakly.

Trifecta

PUPO - Pregnant Until Proven Otherwise —
I imagine printing it on my name badge.

I'm currently four days post-ET (Embryo Transfer)
or FET (Frozen Embryo Transfer if you want to get specific)

but I don't feel pregnant.

Don't want to believe I am either.

I've been there too many times
and it's not pretty when AF arrives.
(Who named it Aunt Flo anyway?)

I respond to a post by WishingOnAStar26 in the forum which reads —

So ladies, who is joining me in being PUPO?

I, MagicHappens33, respond —

I am! Really hoping we're lucky this time!
Don't know if I can do this for much longer. BT due on 2nd November.

Twenty minutes later KT82 announces she's due to test on the second.
We're aiming for a trifecta,
just like LittleFeet77, TanyaT and SunflowerGlow in the October thread.

Fingers tightly crossed, hope hugged in close —
for ourselves and each other.

Pregnant Until Proven Otherwise

PUPO.
Yep, it is my favourite acronym, I decide.
Better than POAS (Pee On A Stick – a home pregnancy test),
but maybe not quite as good as the elusive BFP (Big Fat Positive).
Second favourite then.

I roll it around in my mind, smiling.
Until Proven Otherwise.
Kind of defiant.
Desperate?
Hopeful.
More hopeful than I usually am.

When I'm unpacking the new wine glasses before dinner
I think *PUPO*
and that helps me resist the South Australian merlot on the bench.

I try not to worry
about what will happen next
if this doesn't work.

I don't want surgery –
physicians invading,
peering into me
        with their glinting instruments,
                their gas and their dye.

Please
let this be
third time lucky.

The IVF forum

Is full of women with polycystic ovarian syndrome
or other diagnoses,
      answers that I don't have.

Is full of women who end up with very few embryos
from a stimulated cycle,
      leaving me embarrassed about our frozen stash.

Includes people who are much older than me
who challenge my judgements
      about how old is too old to want a baby.

Includes people who already have multiple children
and want sympathy with their efforts to have their fourth or fifth —
      sympathy I simply can't generate.

Is full of stories of heartbreaking miscarriages
or pregnancy hormone levels that drop
      with each successive test.

      Stories that remind me not to get too excited
      if a Big Fat Positive
      ever
      comes my way.

Planning

Bugger it, let's do it anyway.

But I'm already forty, it's old news! he protests.

But my mind is made up —
he'll get his fortieth party
     no matter if some friends and family can't make it,
       no matter if it's a few months late.
        He needs some laughs,
           we could both do with some ordinary fun.

Before long, he's on board, and it feels good,
this planning something together,
something that will definitely happen,

something we can achieve.

Life of adventure

I hate breaking the news to him,
by text message,
again.

He sends a jokey message back
about me being able to get off my head at his fortieth,
but I know he's devastated.

His life of adventurous trips away
camping and kite-surfing
changed, all but disappeared,
after his friends had babies —

yet he can't seem to join them.

Irony

Maybe the most annoying thing about IVF
is the pregnancy test you have to do
even after enduring a week of raging PMT
and being wearily slapped in the face
at the end of it by a period –

another bright red stop-light.

No-one else would sit down on the toilet
on Day Three of their period to do a pregnancy test,
except those of us who need to follow the clinic's instructions
and test on the date specified, period or no.

We don't approach it like excited women who are new to trying,
eager to see the blue line appear.
No, it's yet another punishing chore,
a horribly predictable lose-lose scenario.

We know the result will either be negative
or in rare cases, worse –
a positive test indicating an ectopic pregnancy
which would need to be terminated
and could lead to bits of our reproductive system
being hacked out in emergency surgery.

How about that?
A negative result brings relief.

Behind the lines

WishingOnAStar26 and KT82 got lucky.

Even on the IVF support forum
everyone except me
seems to be getting pregnant.

A line is a line is a line
KT82 writes determinedly,
posting pics of her faint blue line,
reassuring herself it's really true.

I am happy for them. I really am.

But oh how I long for that thin blue line –
and the prospect of skipping
        across into the First Trimester thread.

I'm glad I didn't join the forum earlier –
it's hard to be the one left behind,
even in cyberspace.

Backdrop

No-one likes to fail
at what they are doing.

Our lives
these last three years
have been acted out
against an ever-present
backdrop
of failure.

Breeze

A light breeze
filtering through my Queensland blue gum,
fanning me
through the open window,

makes all the difference.

Never thought I would

I have embraced science.

Embryos nurtured in a petri dish
by just the right chemical medium.

Now, ethical diamonds synthesized in a lab.

We chose not to marry,
so this ring to celebrate
our ten-year relationship
feels extra special
(even though it was my idea
      and I bought it).

The diamond looks real.
It catches the light,
lifts my spirits
      momentarily.

Sliding it on my finger
I admit

science cannot fix

the trepidation in my heart.

Stopping

A break from IVF.

Aside from one appointment each
with the IVF counsellor and doctor,
we don't need to think about it for a couple of months.

Eight months of assisted conception.

Nothing to show for it
except twenty-one *frosties*
      which is definitely worth raising a glass to.

A pregnant belly would be better.

I get teary thinking about this fierce year
but there is relief
     in stopping

          for a while.

Empty seats

I drive around with a baby capsule
and a toddler's car seat
in the back,
running errands before my sister and her kids
arrive for the party.

These seats should be for our children, Patrick says,
as we ferry platters and glasses to the venue.

I nod, admitting I have felt a tad uncomfortable
knowing they are behind me
wherever I go

those empty seats
occupied by the could've, should've,
might've beens —

the ghosts of our desire.

Three under three

The party is great.
A perfect distraction from IVF
and the whole trying-to-get-pregnant saga.

When I call the nursing home
to speak to my grandmother a few weeks later
she tells me to   *get a wriggle on*
getting married and having kids.

She tells me that after she married they   *let nature run its course*
and within three years
she had three beautiful children under the age of three.

Not sure what to say.

Good for her?

Christmas letter

I often do a Christmas letter
but not this year.

My news?

Employed two new staff,
congratulated by my accountant for excellent book-keeping,
doubled the size of the market stall,
earned good profits at the shop,
worked too hard,
got burnt out,
did eight months of IVF,
survived Ovarian Hyper-Stimulation Syndrome –

no pregnancy to show for it –

organised a ripper of a fortieth birthday party for Patrick
(who this year became a media superstar for a brief time,
the source of all hopes for a low-carbon cattle industry),
celebrated our tenth anniversary of being together,
spent Christmas with family,

played with other people's kids.

Boxing Day newspaper

I have to confess
to being really annoyed
by the standard front page photo
of a baby
born on Christmas Day.

Decimated

I go to give the fruit trees their early morning drink.
The slender branches of both the mango and nectarine trees
        are bent and disfigured.

The lychees have also suffered —
limbs snapped, leaves half-eaten.

The banana trunks are standing
but the leaves stripped.

Damn possums!

I could burst with rage.
I would race in and vent to Patrick
but he's away on Bribie.

I take photos and text them to him with ten anger emojis.

After the rage subsides

> I discern
> a deep
> residual
> sadness.

Prime ministerial support

After one of his staffers reveals that he let her keep
fertility drugs in his parliamentary fridge,
our Catholic Prime Minister makes a public statement
in support of all the *courageous women* doing IVF.

It feels weird to have his support.

Another Liberal minister *comes out* about IVF.

The church hierarchy fumes.

Tragedy

My friend's third child
is born, tragically, asleep.

Now Sienna grieves,
thinking every day of the perfect girl
she made
and lost.

I'm ashamed to remember how sorry for myself I felt,
when she told me she was pregnant,
the same day my sister's waters broke.

My reality gap is not
a baby angel in my hands,
after a long labour knowing
        she was already gone,
after nurturing her full term.

My reality gap is
a continual thwarting of hope,
a constant striving,
a yearning that won't leave,
a life on hold,

enduring
loss after loss after loss
of potential babies

but it's nothing like my friend's
      stark, sudden loss of an actual baby.

A moment of abandon

Sylvia's five-year-old
begs me to jump with her
on her trampoline, a present from Santa.

I bounce around, holding hands, laughing
until I remember the tiny embryo
transferred just yesterday –
the four-celled bundle trying to nestle
into my uterine lining.

I stop,
clamber down, catch my breath,
sip soda water,
try not to admonish myself.

I hope like hell it was hanging on tight,
sticky and settled

or maybe

I bounced it into exactly
the right spot.

Dry season

The day before my period is due.

I wander around the garden inspecting the remaining fruit trees.

Apart from one mandarin,
they are struggling.
It's unusually dry this summer.
Is the clay in the soil baking the roots
like scones in an oven?

We've tried.
A month ago, we spread cow manure,
blood-and-bone, compost,
seaweed spray, black plastic
and mulch
around each tree
to boost nutrients,
conserve soil moisture,
curtail weeds.

I've been watering them a bit
but it's not enough.

The trees and I stare at the arid sky
with mutual glumness.

Sighing

As we unpack boxes of dry goods together,
Evie comments (again)
on how much sighing I've been doing.

It's true.

Everything seems like so much effort.
I lug deep-seated tiredness around.

Infertility is one big sigh.

Signs

Today
all the signs but still no period.

I look out the kitchen window as I rinse my cereal bowl.

The Imperial mandarin has been decimated.

Two unripe, perfectly-formed fruit
lie half-devoured
beneath denuded branches.

A few sad twigs clutch a handful of ripped leaves.

A miserable contrast to the shiny green exuberance of yesterday
when I admired with relief our only thriving fruit tree.

I give up.

The possums win.

Faint blue line

Unable to wait any longer
I give in,
do a Pee On A Stick.
For the very first time
there is a faint test line.

I curse the inconclusiveness of it.

Medication could be the cause.
It takes a week after the last injection to wear off
and in that time, could give a false positive.

For a moment, I imagine
what it would be like to repeat the test tomorrow
and find the blue line has darkened,

Or what it would be like, now, if this timid blue line
was definite, dark, bold, and unequivocally
                                        positive.

Suspense

The next day, Friday,
with still no blood on the scene,
I experience suspense
not dissimilar to a thriller
except it's longer, more drawn out,
and I have to work while it lurks away in the background.

At times it is excruciating
as I have zero energy, am irritable, flat,
feel like I have PMT
but can't be sure.

Moonshine5 tells me not to lose hope,
that many signs of PMT are also signs of pregnancy,
so I allow a ten per-cent flag of hope to flutter.
Or more, maybe,
but I don't admit that to anyone.

I think of Dr Baby-Maker, positioned at my feet,
telling us with a smile
that he would do everything he could at his end to make it work,
that the embryo looked great
— four healthy cells, no fragmentation —
that the ease of getting it through the cervix and into place
was a good sign.

I think of how fit and healthy I am
(after sticking to all my new year's resolutions),
how it's the first transfer we've done after a lengthy holiday,
how it's number four and the odds have to go our way soon,
how it would be such a good way to start off the year,
how it's been forty-nine months and surely
it's bound to happen soon.

In one way it's good excitement,
at least being in the situation where every now and again
I can pause and wonder – am I pregnant?

But it's too dangerous to wonder such things too often,
and mostly it's just plain frustrating,
not knowing,
and not wanting to plan the weekend
because of the not knowing.

Turn out the light

Tonight I Pee On A Stick again.
No blue test line.
The thriller is over
and it's not a happy ending.

Patrick watches *Avengers: End Game*
while I flop in bed, reading Michelle Obama's *Becoming,*
but my heart isn't in it.

We are exhausted.
Defeated.
When we're both under the covers,
he turns out the light
and squeezes my hand.

I'm sorry you're not pregnant.

Me too
I whisper,
tears sliding,
feeling suspended in a bloated emptiness
I've felt too many times before,
realising how much I wanted this to work.

Waiting

And my period still doesn't arrive.

I hate my body.

So cruel,
taunting me
with the signs
of what could've been.

How things can change

I hesitate to say it out loud.
Don't want to jinx it.

How things can change.

All it takes is
      a strong blue line.

Strong line

He won't believe it.
It's just a false positive, he moans, *let me go back to sleep.*
I wave the pee stick in front of his rumpled face.

Look! It's a strong line!
It means I'm pregnant!

The next two days he is weird.
Grumpy, depressed, restless.
His mantra: *Just wait til the blood test.*
Scientists — so damn cautious!

He admits he's not himself,
so used to resigning himself
to the fact that we couldn't get pregnant,
he's struggling to come to terms with the strong possibility
that now   we are actually   pregnant!

At the same time, petrified it won't last.
I feel the same.

Every time I go to the toilet
I check my knickers.

Consider it a small miracle —

        no signs of red.

Hang on

Finally I can allow myself to dream.
That line on the pregnancy urine test
and the absence of Aunt Flo has given me permission for the first time.

I am pregnant! Though I still dare not say the words out loud.
I am highly aware that this dream could end at any time.
I've experienced it before,
read about it in many posts on the forum,
watched women plummet from joy to despair
       with one small bleed
or test results that show pregnancy hormone levels
       diminishing.

I can't really let myself
smile
until I get my blood results in two days' time,
until they tell me the levels are okay.
Hang on, little emby, hang on!

Suddenly I have to revisit my exercise momentum.
Suddenly I know why I've had the munchies.
Suddenly I know what it feels like to have crossed the line
that we've been trying to cross for years!

But it's a strange, nervous time.
If I was religious I'd be praying non-stop.

I allow myself a peek at a pregnancy website
and the First Trimester thread in the IVF forum.

I even work out the due date on an online pregnancy calculator –
see my year planned out for the first time – dangerous thoughts.

Please, please, hang in there!

Nerves

Before work
I have the blood test.

Very excited.
Very nervous.

I play phone tennis with the clinic,
ducking in and out of my training session with a new employee,
finally explain I am awaiting a result.

They call back an hour later
and do what must be the favourite part of their job,
passing on   *the good news.*

It's real!!!
It's happening!!!!
It's positive!!!!
Levels are great!!!!

I'm pregnant!!!!

I call Patrick and can hear
his smile,
his relief,
his excitement,
his abiding fear.

Celebrating

I buy Patrick his favourite treat,
an old-fashioned vanilla slice
from the bakery down the road.

I give it to him that evening
and he laughs, tells me
that after getting The News,
he went to a bakery at lunchtime
and bought himself
a celebratory vanilla slice.

The club

I can't wait —
tell my sister,
my mother,
Sylvia, Holly and Grace.

Instantly and joyously I am welcomed into the motherhood club
I've been standing outside of for years,
watching on.

Now I relish
the sharing of advice,
understanding
and support
for this (almost) universal experience.

We discuss scans,
maternity clothes,
exercise,
diet recommendations,
how to adjust   psychologically.

Entering the First Trimester Thread

I wake and decide
I don't have to wait any longer.
One week since the blood test and I think
     I can believe
        it's real.
Ever since I joined the forum I craved being able to enter
the sacred First Trimester thread.
Even before breakfast I pick up my phone and find it.
My hand shakes slightly.

I made it!!!!! I tap. *I got my BFP a week ago!*
No sign of AF. Hoping not to see her for a very long time!
I give the details, the dates, the levels.

There are four others in here already,
including OzGirl whose pineapples must have worked.
We swap notes on how we're feeling.

This thread has the tone of an end-of-Year-Twelve party —
celebration about graduating,
     tension and nerves about what's ahead.
Will we all make it to the Second Trimester Thread?
We know too well the stats on miscarriages.
We deflect anxiety with posts about pram models, reflux,
iron supplements.
I've never laid eyes on these women

but checking in with them is the highlight of every day. It's the best room I've ever been in.

Swimming as two

As I pull my Speedos on I contemplate what maternity bathers I'll buy
       when my belly swells.
Will I be bold enough to display my burgeoning bump in a stylish bikini?
Will I need ones with heavy-duty support for newly ripe breasts?
Or will I feel self-conscious, stick with baggy t-shirts and shorts
to cover up, hide stretch marks?

I'm allowed to have thoughts like these now.

I head down the beach, stretch on tinted goggles, cap and fins.

    Swim
         and swim.

With every stroke my body smiles.
My neck is neutral, relaxed.
I gaze at the sandy bottom.
Cupped hands glide easily through the water,
pulling down beside my straight, life-bearing torso.
The salt-dense ocean cradles me.
Every third stroke I rotate hips and shoulders,
     open my chest, breathe.
I flutter-kick rhythmically, power coming from my hips.
My arms extend energetically,
     embracing momentum.
I am streamlined,

strong,
one with my body again.

I am conscious that inside me,
a tiny new person
      is forming
      floating.

He or she will grow up here in the Bay,
a bonnet-topped beach baby
Patrick and I can introduce to the cheeky lorikeets,
splash with in the clear shallows,
perch behind us as we ride bikes along the Esplanade,
        finally

    a baby of our own.

Gagging on plain crackers

When I start complaining about nausea,
Patrick is more excited
than sympathetic.

I come across a comment by OzGirl in the First Trimester thread
and read it out to him —

Every day that I look greener and come closer to vomiting,
Bloke is even more pleased.
When I nearly fainted at work (how embarrassing)
he was just about ecstatic.

Patrick laughs *I know how he feels.*

Nausea equals proof
      to my darling scientist —
gagging on plain crackers has never been more welcome.

Duds

Things I bought when we started trying to have a baby:
non-alcoholic champagne (fancy name for sparkling grape juice)
and a family-sized tent for Patrick,
for his thirty-seventh birthday, to show him
that we could still enjoy the outdoors
                                    with kids in tow.

The fake champagne lurked on the bottom shelf
reminding me of our predicament
every time I opened the fridge to get a glass of milk, some jam.

One day soon I'll be able to celebrate by drinking that
I would tell myself,
until the years dragged on.
Two years in, I decided enough was enough
and served it to a pregnant friend.

The tent was dragged out once
for a camping trip
but it was so big he was embarrassed,
hasn't unpacked it since.

Maybe it won't be such a dud gift after all.

Balance

There's a baby growing inside me!

I have to balance the need
to rapidly learn about
doing all the right things
to ensure successful foetus development
while at the same time trying not to get too carried away —

don't count your chickens ...

Jelly bean

The seven-week scan.
If it goes well, we'll graduate from this clinic.
Dr Baby-Maker must have witnessed a spectrum of responses –
quiet tears, torrential sobbing, manic exclamations of joy.

Our eyes are fixed on the screen,
trying hard to translate
the grainy black and white language of my womb.

We see a small, dark jelly bean
pulsating.

Doctor announces

Jade and Patrick, that's your baby,
　　　　　there's its heart beating, see

pointing his magic wand
at the definite, visible pulsing.

We grin at each other wildly, release our breaths,
inwardly revel in happiness and relief.
He does the measurements, tells us   *It's perfect.*

Thank-you, Dr Baby-Maker.
Thank-you.

Lucky

We are finally in the parents-to-be elevator.
Each level is new and marvellous.

I am ridiculously excited about buying a pram.
Research the options online for days.

We have learnt so much we didn't want to know,
felt so much we didn't want to feel,
done so much we didn't plan on doing,

but in the end we are beyond
lucky
and we know it.

The sweetest thing
is Patrick's hand on my belly,
feeling for movement,
the tiny heart tapping —

our new drumbeat.

4.

Epilogue

She hands me the test tube through the lab window,
confirms twenty embryos float in the diaphanous fluid —
        invisible   but there …

How long did it take for them to die? I quaver.

Hard to tell, they've been on the bench a while,
but I'd say seconds.

I posted the form a month ago,
gave the order
to take them out.

Today, after dropping our daughter at kindy,
Patrick, our two-year-old son and I
drive to Mount Walsh National Park.
We hike to Utopia Falls,
through cabbage palms, stately water-gums
and thousands of small yellow butterflies dotting the gully.

We clamber down slippery granite rocks to a small waterfall.
Pull the stopper,
flush them all into the clear gelid water
running through the rocks, ferns, leaves —

these cells that first came to be
inside the warmth of our bodies,
sperm and eggs who met and fused
in a plastic petri dish,
transformed into precious zygotes,
potential brothers and sisters
of our two glorious, same-batch children.

Crouching by the stream I rinse the tube and the lid over and over,
say goodbye to these quiescent possibilities
whose lives ended at the microscopic stage,
the I've-got-enough-children-now-I-don't-need-you-stage.

I'm sorry
the drugs overstimulated,
conned my follicles into developing a near-record number of eggs.
In laboratory conditions our sperm and eggs
lost their usual reticence
and you all came to be
in a joyous explosion of potential.

That phone call telling us the embryo count —
such astonishing relief,
instant thriving hope
and, behind it all, unacknowledged dread
of finding ourselves here.

We never wanted to play God.

We can't bear to give you away to other couples
not knowing how you might be treated
                         or mistreated.

We can't bear to let anyone
practice needling you,
extracting your chromosomes for experiments.

My heart expands and aches
for all twenty of you
allowed to grow for forty-eight hours
then vitrified,
kept in straws, for years,
in tanks of liquid nitrogen.

If you had come into being naturally inside me
at Day Two you wouldn't yet have made it past the fallopian tubes
into my uterus,
you may never have attached there,
blossomed into blastocysts, embryos, foetuses, babies …

Now you are thawed
released into the care of this clear cascading grave.

We let you go   never to know
if you would have nestled into my uterine wall
like so many before you failed to do.

Tears slip with you

down these granite rocks.
Grief for the lives you might have lived.

Thank-you   (such a slight word)
for kindling hope in my most ruinous days,
for providing
          from your tribe
our two shining children.

See your brother is here,
wondering at a wet stone he holds in his hands,
oblivious to the act he is witnessing.

He and his sister were both conceived at the same time,
both frozen.

They have been brought to life,
through my body, into my arms
and you have not.

But I will keep the memory of you all
cryopreserved.

Trudging back up the dry rainforest path
I barely notice the pair of wonga pigeons foraging
as I grimly recall
thick needles, thin needles, nose sprays,
transvaginal probes,
triggering injections,

blood tests,
the egg retrieval operation,
embryo transfers,
cataclysmic troughs and crests.

When we get home
I place the rinsed-out test tube
      and its IVF packet in the kitchen bin,
turn around slowly,
fill the resting kettle.

Acknowledgements

A compilation version of 'Weight of expectation' and 'Whale watching' won First Prize in the Fellowship of Australian Writers Tasmania Poetry Prize 2021, while 'Name games' and 'The dance' together were Highly Commended. 'Intimacy' and 'The poise of liquid nitrogen' were together Commended in the Woorilla Poetry Prize 2021.

'Happy accidents' was published in the *Australian Poetry Journal Volume* 12.1, 2022. 'Mother's work' was published in a different version titled 'the spare room' in *Women's Work – A collection of Contemporary Women's Poetry* anthology edited by Libby Hathorn and Rachel Bailey, Pax Press, 2013.

Different versions of 'Flatness', 'Pudgy legs', 'Bleeding', 'Splashing out', 'Been watching too many documentaries?', 'Barren' and 'Empty seats' were published as a group with the title 'Vacant Seats' in *The Sky Falls Down – An Anthology of Loss* edited by Terry Whitebeach and Gina Mercer, Ginninderra Press, 2019.

A different version of 'Things that make me happy' was part of the 2013 Poets and Painters project and exhibited at the Bett Gallery along with an artwork by Amanda Davies.

This project has been assisted by the Australian Government through the Australia Council, its arts funding and advisory body. I am eternally grateful for Dr Gina Mercer's insightful mentorship and editing of this verse novel. She proved to be a staunchly supportive and inspiring ally on this quest.

Thanks also to Liz Winfield, Melinda Smith, Jane Williams and members of my poetry circle for their invaluable support and feedback. Thanks to Oasis Women Poets, Robyn Mathison, the Fellowship of Australian Writers Tasmania and TasWriters. Thanks also to my fabulous friends Jen Welch, Jen Lorrimar-Shanks, Pen Clark, Susanna Fishburn, Kelly Pettit and Sally Casey who were my first readers and who responded with warm encouragement. Thanks to Millie Pardoe for checking over the health food shop details. Thanks to Esther Ottaway for being such a wonderful poetry friend and ally, and for generously supporting this project and others.

Thanks to Jen Welch, Ida Welch, Susanna Fishburn and Greer Carland for applying their creative talents to workshopping ideas for the cover and enormous thanks to Jen Lorrimar-Shanks who designed the final cover images and patiently and skilfully crafted the cover layout.

Thanks to Fiona Johnson from Beyond Words Literary Agency for believing in and championing this work.

I am sincerely grateful to Ralph Wessman from Walleah Press who has always supported me and my writing and who remained committed to bringing this book to publication. The altruistic contribution of his time and skills is deeply appreciated.

I'm grateful for the members of the creative writing group I facilitate at The Hobart Clinic for sharing the inspiration and healing properties of poetry with me.

Thanks to my family for always being there for me, especially my mother and sister. Thanks to my wonderful husband Jeremy for his love and patience as I worked on this project. This story is fictional but inspired by our own experience of infertility. We are grateful to Dr Bill Watkins and TasIVF for their help.

This book is dedicated to our two beautiful children, Katie and Rory, who bring much love and joy into our lives.

When writing this book, I was conscious that many readers may have been through a fraught fertility journey of their own. Every journey is different and I know how lucky we were to have the outcome that we did. I especially want to acknowledge the pain and suffering and send my deepest sympathy to all those reading whose journeys did not work out as hoped. My hope is that this book can at least add to the community's understanding about some aspects of the struggle.

About the author

Susan Austin is a poet, eco-socialist activist and occupational therapist. She facilitates group programs, including a creative writing program, in a mental health clinic in Hobart. Her first poetry collection *Undertow* was published by Walleah Press in 2012. An earlier version was awarded First Commended in the Best First Book category of the IP Picks 2011 competition. In 2020 she was awarded a Career Development Grant by the Australia Council for the Arts to work with Dr Gina Mercer on this book.

Susan has been a guest performer at two Tasmanian Poetry Festivals, Seasonal Poets (Hadley's Hotel), the Festival of Golden Words (now the Tamar Valley Writers Festival) and the Tasmanian Writers Festival. She has judged the WILPF Eve Masterman Peace Poetry Prize, been featured on Radio National's Poetica program and has had work widely published in newspapers and journals. She can be found at www.susanaustinpoetry.com.au and as Susan Austin Poet on Facebook.

Australian Government

Australia Council for the Arts

www.ingramcontent.com/pod-product-compliance
Lightning Source LLC
Chambersburg PA
CBHW020007140726
47904CB00018B/2000